Little Girl
with
Crooked Bangs

L YNN R AE D AVIDSON

ISBN 978-1-64458-755-3 (paperback)
ISBN 978-1-64458-756-0 (digital)

Christian Faith Publishing, Inc.
832 Park Avenue
Meadville, PA 16335
www.christianfaithpublishing.com

Printed in the United States of America

This book is dedicated to all the women who influenced my life especially:

My mother, Mildred, who taught me life lessons during my formative years with love and a hearty dose of "sisu." She handled family adversity, pain, and sorrow by cleaning the house, scrubbing floors and walls, and pushing forward. She had courage to tackle new adventures and never looked back.

My sister Janet, who was my ultimate cheerleader. From my birth to adulthood she encouraged me to believe that I could do most anything within reason. Even when her body was hurting, she encouraged others.

My daughters, Robyn, Brooke Rae, and Amy Lynn, who have given their mother forever joy. I thank God every day for the honor of nurturing them and watching their lives evolve into the most beautiful of butterflies.

My mother-in-law Jackie, who lived by the philosophy when life gives you lemons, make lemonade and have a party. A happy and positive spirit radiated in her gift of hospitality.

And to the man who made life worth living:

My husband Russell, who loved me even when I could not love myself. I know that God destined us to be together from a very young age. We grew up together and now grow old together. I believe that the best is yet to be.

Special thanks to Maime Hjulberg and Arden and Rudolph Johnson for family historical and factual content. This book tells a story and the author is not responsible for the correctness of its contents.

INTRODUCTION

OUR LIVES CONSIST OF MOMENTS. As one moment ends, another begins. Add them all together, and they become our story.

Everyone has a story that needs to be told. Daily experiences bring valuable teaching, usually designed for personal growth. As each moment unfolds, it becomes a channel for metamorphosis—physically, mentally, and spiritually.

The transformation may occur slowly, but, inevitably, change happens. When moments blend together, they create our life's story. Our genetic makeup and also the environment—our home, church, community, work, and school—greatly influence us. Sharing and journaling them help us to understand ourselves which will, in turn, help us to understand others.

In his book *Wherever You Go, There You Are*, author Jon Kabat-Zinn introduces the reader to mindfulness meditation in everyday life. He shows us that "mindfulness," the heart of Buddhist meditation, is universal and of deep practical benefit.

Our minds are such that we are often more asleep than awake to the unique beauty and possibilities of each moment as it unfolds. In the beginning, from within our mother's womb, until we draw our last breath, we are part of a beautiful plan.

Metamorphosis occurs in our life much like that of the monarch butterfly. The butterfly's striking colors and patterns only become apparent as it slowly squirms and wiggles out from the cocoon. Likewise, with us, inner beauty and full potential often times take form only after a difficult struggle or painful trial.

Therefore, we need to awaken to our moments and understand the slow process of emerging from within the cocoon. As you read my story, I challenge you to recall some of yours. Write them down both the joyful, as well as the painful. They are the reason "you are." Because you cannot escape yourself.

"For wherever you go, there you are."

The longing for completion and fulfillment culminate only after we start recalling from the very beginning.

This Moment

We have this moment to hold in our hands,
And to touch as it slips through our fingers like sand;
Yesterday's gone, and tomorrow may never come,
But we have this moment today.

—Bill Gaither

CHAPTER 1

Along the Road of Life

Behold, I am going to send an angel before
you to guard you along the way
and to bring you to a place which I have prepared.
—Exodus 23:20 (NKJV)

FLUFFY SNOW SWIRLED ACROSS THE *highway like cumulus clouds drifting across the sky. Lynn carefully navigated the maroon-colored Plymouth van through the busy streets of Superior, Wisconsin. The vehicle had been delivered two months earlier with an odometer reading of only thirteen miles. Although, technically, the van belonged to Avon Corporation, it was the first new set of wheels Lynn called hers and hers alone. Previously, she drove a tan four-door Impala of her parents and later shared a pearl-white sporty two-door Cutlass Supreme with her husband, Russ.*

How excited she had been to get a new vehicle, and today, Lynn headed south to Danbury for a three-o'clock appointment at the Hole in the Wall Café. Centrally located in northwestern Wisconsin, it was easily accessible to clients. Often, Lynn met women at the quaint restaurant, where the food was delicious and inexpensive. She always picked up the tab from those meetings, never capping the $2,000 monthly expense account that she was allotted.

The major purpose for the Danbury meeting was recruitment. Lynn would separately interview two perspective sales associates. She hoped each woman would meet Avon's criteria, and thus join her district sales force of 280 associates and growing weekly.

It was all about the numbers, and at the last corporate conference in Chicago, the divisional manager dangled a golden carrot as an incentive to districts that met recruiting goals. An all-expense-paid trip to Las Vegas would be awarded to every manager who added at least ten new associates to their sales force. Lynn was confident her personal goal would be reached before next month's deadline. She thrived on challenges. That's why she was hired.

Snowfall chilled the February afternoon with gray skies overhead. The van's wheels plowed steadily through light drifts along Highway 35 just south of Superior. Lynn daydreamed of warmer days, basking in the desert sun of Nevada—never once anticipating any danger traveling. She believed that she was in control. Her new vehicle was equipped with front-wheel drive, airbags, and antilock brakes. Lynn was a safe, competent driver. Besides, God was on her side, protecting her, right?

For as long as she could remember, Lynn trusted in the fact that someone would always keep her safe.

*****

In the beginning, Ray, her dad, had been there from inception. The two had a strong father-daughter bond. Lynn adored her father, and she knew that he adored her.

Ray's protective shield of love for his family grew from the examples set by those who came before him. He was the second son of Andrew Edwin and Esther Sophia (Sjoblad) Juntunen. He teased incessantly yet loved his seven brothers and six sisters. They were a very typical farming family, theirs being one of the largest in Thomson Township.

As a young boy, Ray was the sidekick of his grandfather Joseph. Early on, his father, Ed, instructed the lad to watch and learn horsemanship from Joseph. The elder man had a gentle way of guiding the huge workhorses. He spoke to them, and they understood and obeyed his commands…well, most of the time.

Story be told, there was one day when they didn't. The autumn morn began early by milking the cows. After that, plowing needed to be done at the Moilanens. The eighty acres were purchased in 1920 from Elsa's younger sister, Vaapu Moilanen, and her husband. A small creek meandered through its rolling hills, and the soil was rich and fertile.

The property, only two miles from the Juntunen homestead, was planted for oats every other year, following proper crop rotation. Autumnal plowing would prepare the soil for seeds to sow in the spring.

After morning milking and barn chores, Ed instructed his twelve-year-old son, Raymond.

"The field is dry enough to plow. Take the team and go with Grandpa to the Moilanens," the father said to his son.

As usual, Raymond obeyed and bridled up the horses while Grandpa Joseph asked Ray's oldest sister Bernice to pack a lunch: bread, *villia* (Finn word for fermented product much like yogurt), along with a can of sardines. Water and a quart jar of buttermilk *piimä* provided their beverages for the day.

The boy and his grandfather rode with the wagon, and massive horses west on Harney Road. Once they got to the field, Ray hitched the Percherons to the plow from the hay shed. The team lunged forward and began to turn over the rich dirt. For several hours, they plodded up and down the rows, stopping only when necessary to move a boulder with the crowbar. Once in a while, a mouse scurried from his upended home, as greedy gulls hovered over the unearthed soil in search of food.

After several hours of plowing, Ray became very hungry but patiently waited until his grandfather gave a nod and slight grin to his grandson. That was the cue Ray needed. Quickly, he led the horses to the nearby creek for water and a short rest. Then under a cluster of weeping willows, the old grandfather and his ravenous grandson ate their lunch from the base of a hollow tree stump.

The two took turns eating from the sardine can and tearing hunks from the half round of rye bread *liimpa*. The fresh bread tasted so good that Ray ate more than his share and washed it down with warm buttermilk, *piimä*. Grandpa didn't mind. He knew the boy was growing up, while he was only growing old.

After lunch, Raymond hitched up Pat and Dan, ready to finish plowing. Suddenly, he felt his throat tighten and stomach roll. He swallowed, but it was too late. Vomit spewed from his mouth and nose. The smell and taste of sardines seared his nostrils and parched his tongue. Grandpa just looked away and grinned slightly. He knew that the boy had eaten too much, too fast, and nature took over. For several years after that incident, Ray politely refused to eat sardines.

An upset stomach was no excuse to quit plowing. Raymond resumed shortly after the vomiting subsided. Later that afternoon, grandson and grandfather finished tilling the large field. Ray unhooked the plow from the horses and replaced it with the short wagon. The boy and old man climbed up on the wagon and headed for home.

Pat and Dan trotted along the Harney Road toward Puotinen's farm. It had been a good day's work, the old man mused, even if the boy had puked *"oksentaaed."* That'll teach him not to stuff himself, he thought, as he proudly looked over at his grandson. Ed was right about Ray. He was eager to learn all about horse whispering and about handling these mammoth farmworkers.

As if the horses sensed nearing the stable, they picked up their pace from a trot to a gallop. Their large hoofs clicked the loose gravel on the Harney Road, going faster and faster. Raymond pulled on the reins with all his might in an attempt to slow down the team. Nothing worked.

The closer the duo got to the barn, the faster they galloped. Grandpa hollered, "Ho, there, ho, ho!" Ray knew the team was out of control and there was only one option. As the farm came into sight, he hollered to his grandfather, "Jump!" and flew off the wagon into the ditch. Grandpa followed, his short legs and long arms flying through the air.

When he hit the ground, Joseph looked over at his grandson to see if he was hurt. The boy looked at his grandpa to see if the old man was still alive.

Joseph rolled over from his back and smirked as he spoke, "*Voi, voi, voi*, Raymontti, you're not as good of a horseman as I thought!"

The two laughed as they watched dust swirling in the air. Farther ahead, the runaway horses thundered to the stable. As abruptly as the large beasts bolted, they suddenly stopped at the gate. They knew they were home.

Raymond learned three lessons that day.

1. Sardines leave an awful taste in your mouth, especially when they come back up.
2. If your team of workhorses is going to bolt, there's nothing to do but jump and let 'em go.
3. Much like the draft horses that galloped back to the stable's security, Ray understood that "there's no place like home."

CHAPTER 2

Come Away with Me

Oh God, that you would bless me indeed and enlarge my
territory, that your hand would be with me and that you
would keep me from harm, that I may not cause pain.
And God granted him that which he requested.
—1 Chronicles 4:10 (NIV)

JOSEPH JUNTUNEN AND ELSA JULIANA Pykkonen were both born in
Suomussalmi, Finland. Joseph came into this world on February 24,
1859, to Heikki (Henrick) Juntunen and his wife Anna Seppanen.
Joseph grew to be a short man in stature with long arms, though
certainly not short on ambition and courage. Legend has it that he
could pick up an object from the ground without hardly bending his
knees. This proved quite valuable when potato picking.

Elsa was one of ten children born on May 18, 1861, to Jonas
and Elsa Pykkonen. As a young woman, she had petite, dainty fea-
tures, thick dark hair, and bewitching blue eyes. Her tiny frame made
it possible for Joseph to encircle her waist with his large hands. Witty
Elsa had a great sense of humor which Joseph found irresistible, and
before long the two fell in love.

Times were difficult during the latter part of the nineteenth
century. The Russian, Swedish, and Norwegian governments vied for
controlling much of northern Finland. For centuries, Finnish society
consisted of nobility, clergy, burghers (middle class), and peasants.

Class tensions often arose between property owners (White forces) and landless farm, forest, and factory workers (Red forces), who wanted a socialist state.

Many of the Finnish people heard about the opportunities in America and considered leaving because of the unrest and famine. When they gathered together, their conversation evolved around crossing the Atlantic Ocean and finding prosperity in the New World.

Earlier some of Elsa's family sailed across the ocean in the ship's steerage and wrote home about the traumatic experience.

Elsa shared this news with Joseph. "Did you know, Joseph, that people were like cows in a large hold below deck? It was filthy and smelled awful!"

"Voi, voi," puffed Joseph in the Finnish term for "My, oh my!" Then he continued, "It must've been so terrible going all the way across the big water."

Most on board were seasick and afflicted with dysentery. Still weeks after arriving, these stalwart immigrants wrote lengthy letters back to the homeland encouraging other relatives to make the difficult journey to the United States just as they had done.

Back in Finland, young Joseph with great interest reread the letters and listened intently when the men spoke of embarking on this long journey onboard a ship. He knew it would not be easy. He carefully weighed his options. Several factors influenced his decision.

First of all, there was an established custom stating that the eldest son would inherit the family farm. Joseph was the second son of Heikki and Anna. The farm would be promised to his older brother. Joseph would have to find a livelihood elsewhere.

Secondly, he wanted to escape the Russian dominance of Finland. The Russians were often in conflict with neighboring countries. When Joseph reached the age of twenty-one, most likely, he would be drafted to fight in a Russian war. He wanted at all costs to avoid military service to the Russian Empire.

Finally, Joseph would not receive his parents' blessing to marry Elsa, because of unwritten rules regarding the Finnish class system. Property owners were strongly discouraged from marrying landless renters. The Juntunens were middle-class landowners, while Elsa's father was not.

Several years earlier, Jonas Pykkonen lost his property in Kuresuvanto because he could not pay the high taxes imposed by the Russian and Norwegian governments. The faltering economy made times very difficult for people living in the northern regions. There were several years of harsh weather followed by a famine. These were lean years with minimum work for Jonas. The family experienced extreme poverty. In order to stay alive, they ate trapped birds, boiled straw and tree bark. Eventually, Elsa's mother died of starvation.

Taking all these factors into consideration, Elsa and Joseph realized there wasn't a promising future for them in Finland. Together, they agreed to leave their birthplace and planned a strategy. The next day, they wrote letters to family members, who had already emigrated to America. They waited and waited for mail from the United States.

"Joseph, it has been many weeks since we wrote to the Moilanens in Michigan. Do you think they got our letter?" The young woman sighed.

"You must be patient, Elsa. The ships carry mail, and it takes many days for a steamship to cross the ocean twice to the United States and back."

When a letter finally arrived, the couple was overjoyed by the positive response from relatives who sent money for passage across the Atlantic. With mixed emotions, the pilgrims left their native land, their families, and friends, and traveled to the port of Trondheim, Norway. They waited for three days before the steamer arrived and docked at the port. After unloading cargo and freight, the crew prepared to launch the next day.

Determined to make better lives for themselves, Elsa and Joseph set sail in third class to the "Promised Land" on Wednesday, June 7, 1880. Elsa was accompanied by her uncle, as it was unacceptable for women to travel alone, and since she was not married to Joseph, a male relative was required to "watch over" the young lady.

Homemade crusty rye bread *muccara*, a Finnish term for bologna; hard cheese; and pickled fish were their staples for the transatlantic voyage which took twelve days. Unfortunately, Elsa experienced seasickness and didn't eat much of the rations, while her uncle and fiancé came down with dysentery. After docking in New York, they collected their scant belongings.

At last, the fearless passengers, along with five hundred Finns, Norwegians, and Swedes, disembarked the steamer and its dismal conditions in steerage. Then with travel documents in hand and wobbly sea legs, they made their way onto Ellis Island to legally enter the United States.

Joseph and Elsa looked at each other; then on cue their eyes peered up at the blue sky above. They were giddy yet a little frightened as their feet stepped onto American soil.

The trio could hardly believe that their sailing days had finally ended. Elsa joked to Joseph and her uncle, "Pinch me. Am I dreaming?"

"*Ei, Elsa,*" her uncle replied in his native tongue, "no." Then in broken English, he continued, "You in USA!"

Their grasp of the English language left much to be desired. Still it appeared that most of their fellow passengers were in the "same boat."

Anticipation and excitement bubbled up from within Joseph and Elsa as they ventured by train northwest as far as the Upper Peninsula of Michigan. Many Finns who came from the Suomussalmi area went to work in the Michigan copper mines. Consequently, it was logical that Elsa and Joseph would first go there to seek employment. Both agreed that once they saved enough money, they would marry.

Joseph was hired by a Michigan mining company but quickly discovered he couldn't adjust to the working conditions. He was a farmer from Suomussalmi unaccustomed to copper mining. Yet for the time being, "*sisu,*" the word used to typify the Finnish spirit of being "brave, resilient, determined with inner strength and grit" sustained him. He knew the job was only temporary.

Meanwhile, in a nearby town, Elsa found work as a housekeeper. She enjoyed cooking and visiting with others. Unfortunately, she couldn't speak a word of English. Instead of conversing with others in the household, she talked Finn to the dog. Every Sunday, unhappy and lovesick, young Joseph walked several miles to be with Elsa. Together, they dreamed about their future.

During those first two years in the United States, Joseph saved enough from his meager earnings to merit taking a bride. One Sunday, he announced to Elsa, "I am tired of walking every Sunday to visit with you for such a short time, then walking back to the mining camp. Haven't we saved enough money? And how much is enough? Let's get married, Elsa, as soon as we can."

The next weekend, the two went by rail to Duluth and were married by a Presbyterian minister. A Finnish Lutheran pastor couldn't be found. The year was 1882.

Following the brief ceremony, the newlyweds immediately found a restaurant where they ate heartily. Food was always an important part of any celebration. Their next stop was to a general store. Elsa bought a bolt of cotton fabric, and Joseph found a warm woolen cap which fit well over his ears. Their wedding night was spent at the train depot. Since the train to Canada departed at 6 AM, the couple deemed it frivolous to get a room for a few short hours. Instead, they spread the fabric over and under them as a makeshift bed on the depot floor…a very unusual bridal suite. Early the next morning, the train arrived and transported them to Thunder Bay for a very short honeymoon.

The new Mr. and Mrs. Juntunen returned to Michigan with a plan to work hard and save as much money as possible. Their dream was to eventually buy a small piece of property to farm and raise a family. Yet at the end of the day, the young couple realized that they missed their family, and once in a while, Joseph questioned his decision to leave Finland. Despite his ambivalence, doubts were erased when he looked over at his lovely bride lying beside him.

A few months passed, and Joseph left the copper mines. Fortunately, he found work on the Canadian Pacific Railroad which was being built in order to quickly ship lumber and copper out of the area. Inexpensive rooms with hot meals for the new settlers were in great demand in the Upper Peninsula. Industrious Elsa and another woman seized the opportunity and opened a boarding house. The rooms were rarely vacant, and the simple yet tasty suppers were welcomed by the mostly male tenants, who were hungry and tired after a long day's work.

At the end of the week, Joseph and Elsa climbed the stairs to their tiny room in the boarding house. They sat on the bed and counted their money. Then they stuffed the cash into the small cigar box and hid it under a loose floorboard for safekeeping. Very soon, they'd be ready to leave Northern Michigan to replace Copper Country for farmers' country.

Cooperatives sprung up in the United States, and many Finns joined, but not the Juntunens. Joseph thought co-ops were socialistic Red movements similar to those in Finland. Therefore, he wanted no part of the co-ops. Needless to say, buying a piece of property was a very high priority to Joseph Juntunen. He knew that in the old country owning land was a sign of prosperity. Those beliefs followed him to the United States and later to his grave.

During the thirty months in Upper Michigan, the frugal husband and wife managed to save $2,000 which was quite an accomplishment. The money was equivalent today to about $50,000. After Elsa's mother collapsed and died from starvation near the town of Suomussalmi, the young woman remained vigilant in her efforts to climb out of the snares of poverty. After all, hadn't she heard that America was the land of opportunity?

Still Joseph was very homesick. He wondered aloud to his wife, "Maybe we should use our savings and go back home?"

Elsa countered, "You are a foolish man, Joseph, and I want no part of that."

She had worked too hard to throw it all away on steerage tickets back to a country which had only impoverished her family.

One evening, after everyone in the boarding house was asleep, the couple tiptoed down the creaky steps and outside onto the porch. Side by side, they sat on the wooden bench and bowed their heads.

"Dear God," Joseph began, "please show us the way. We are young and need your guidance."

Elsa remained silent, but in her heart, she knew she could never return to the harsh conditions she had known back in Finland. She prayed her husband would come into agreement with her.

The next morning was Sunday, and after preparing breakfast for the boarding house tenants, the two dressed for church. The hem on Elsa's well-worn dress was raveling, and Joseph's only white dress shirt was no longer white but a grayish yellow.

Elsa and Joseph walked to the small cabin in town that was used for church services. Some of the men smelled of stale tobacco smoke and cheap whiskey from the night before. Their wives, hoping the sermon would ignite a fire in their menfolk, pushed them along to the wooden chairs near the front.

Joseph and Elsa hardly noticed. They were preoccupied with decision-making and barely heard the message by the lay preacher. The Laestadian movement in the United States had reached the Calumet Peninsula, but this day, the stern sermon fell on deaf ears.

Instead, as parishioners exited the building, Joseph stopped to help an old man see-sawing his way down the steps. The old-timer, whose knees were worn from heavy work in the mines, was very appreciative and spoke softly to Joseph, "You are a kind young man. May the Lord give you increase. May you be blessed of the Lord, Maker of heaven and earth. The heavens are the heavens of the Lord, but the earth he has given to the sons of men."

The old man was quoting Psalm 115. As Elsa and Joseph listened, they knew his words were a confirmation. The time had come to leave Michigan and move on.

One week later, Joseph with hard earned money in sox and Elsa on his arm, said good bye to the Upper Peninsula. By rail the twenty-something husband and wife traveled west along the shore of Lake Superior until they reached its furthermost point of Duluth Minnesota.

The rail yard was noisy and dirty, but the young couple didn't mind. After stepping off the train, they waited for their trunk to be lifted from the baggage section. That trunk held all their earthly belongings. Their clothes protected the coffee cups and saucers, a wedding gift from Jussi Niemi and his wife Hilda. Also, a colorful handwoven rug and a Bible were stuffed around the trunk's edge.

The two heard of a small boarding house in Duluth's western hillside managed by Finns. Joseph and Elsa made their way to its door. The landlady had one room available for the week. Two meals were included with renting the modestly furnished sleeping quarters. The weary travelers quickly agreed to stay while contemplating their next move. The woman told them about a nearby diner where each morning several Finnish men met for coffee and conversation. Joseph made the decision to pay them a visit after getting a good night's sleep.

Once in the small room, Joseph sat on the wooden chair next to the bed. He slowly pulled his right boot off, then his left boot. He stretched his toes and began to peel off his wool sox one at a time. Inside the sox, the man hid hundreds of dollars. Earlier, he decided it was a safe place to keep the bills. Now he regretted the fact. Yet he concluded that although the money was damp and stinky, the currency hadn't lost its value. Carefully, Joseph placed each bill to air out and dry on top of the dresser. He and his wife needed that cash no matter what course they'd take.

Before purchasing two transatlantic fares back to Finland, Joseph considered his wife's ambivalence about returning to a country where she only remembered poverty and heartache. He decided in the meantime to sleep on it. When a new day dawned, he'd stop by the coffee shop and talk to the locals.

The bright sun rose over Lake Superior around 6:00 a.m. *What a beautiful sight*, thought Joseph who was already up, dressed, and peering out the second-story window of the boarding house. Elsa, barely awake, lay exhausted from the long train ride and lack of sleep. For most of the night, she listened to either the bellering men at the seedy tavern across the street or to her snoring husband.

Unlike his wife, Joseph was well rested and anxious to meet the Finns if only to hear news from the homeland. He left his yawning Elsa and hurriedly walked five blocks to the Third Street Coffee Shop. Arriving early, he sat down at a round wooden table and ordered coffee from a hefty waitress named Olga. Then he kept glancing over to the door and back to his pocket watch. Finally, two middle-aged men walked in and looked in Joseph's direction.

Joseph spoke first the common Finnish greeting, "*Hyvaa paivaa*," as he stood up from his chair.

The two men smiled and walked over to shake Joseph's large rough hand. As they exchanged greetings, Olga stood by waiting to take their order. Soon, she returned with hot coffee and biscuits. The three men barely noticed as they jabbered nonstop.

The men told Joseph about a small Finnish settlement fifteen miles south of Duluth and about a Christian man, Albert Mikola, who was selling his farm and moving to New York Mills. Joseph thought this place might be exactly what he and Elsa envisioned. After asking a few more questions about the farmstead in Thomson Township, Joseph jumped up from his chair. He was anxious to share with his wife everything he had been told.

He paid Olga for the coffee and biscuits, then thanked the men, and excused himself. Joseph ran the five blocks back to the boarding house faster than a Helsinki minute.

Huffing and puffing, he could hardly get the words out of his mouth, "Elsa, I want to take the train and go look at this farm that's for sale."

Elsa laughed out loud, "I've never seen you so excited!"

"Well, my sweet wife, this might be just the farm we've been looking for!"

Two days later, Joseph stepped off the train in Harney and walked until he reached the bridge which crossed over the Midway River. He stood there in awe. The surrounding area reminded him of his native land. Birch and poplar trees grew along the edges of the pasture. A wooded area to the east was filled with spruce and cedar trees.

Joseph slowly made his way down the narrow dirt road toward the farmhouse where its owner was waiting. Upon meeting Mr. Mikola and exchanging pleasantries with him, Joseph was shown the buildings. A four-room log house with a loft, a sauna, barn, and a blacksmith shop would be sold along with eighty acres that hugged the banks of the river.

"The two cows and horse will come with the farm. I don't want to bother taking them to New York Mills. Why don't you look around and let me know what you think?"

According to legend, it was then that Joseph turned to the west and leisurely walked along the winding river and surveyed the landscape. He leaned against the wooden gate and looked over the fields, the river, and buildings. He recalled the prophetic words spoken to him less than a week earlier by the old man at the church. God whispered to Joseph deep down in his soul, and he knew this land was to be his and his descendants.

A purchase agreement was made with a shake of hands, and in July of 1885, Joseph and Elsa bought the Mikola farmstead. Instead of going back to Finland, as once thought, they followed God's leading and became Minnesota landowners. They used their entire savings of $2,000 to buy the property.

Joseph was determined to make a better life for Elsa and himself…better than that which they'd left behind. Together, they began this new adventure and never looked back.

Ten days later the young couple moved into the farmhouse. Their arms and legs ached from scrubbing floors and walls, as well as, unpacking their sparse belongings. After the long day of moving in, Elsa made a request. "Please get the fire going in the sauna stove. I want to take a nice, hot sauna before bed, Joseph."

The man honored his wife's request and before long the two were perched on the highest bench taking steam.

Breaking the silence Joseph remarked, "We are blessed, Elsa, we are finally home."

"*Yo, yo, aviomies,*" yes, yes husband, she sighed.

Finns don't often express their emotions. Although during this inaugural sauna time, the two were exhausted and overwhelmed by their good fortune. They were well aware that God directed them to America, then to Duluth where Joseph first heard of the Mikola farmstead. What followed became their first real estate transaction in the small Finnish hamlet of Thomson Township.

*****

Years passed quickly for the couple, and they were blessed with twelve children of whom two died in their infancy. Along with the births of children, came land acquisitions, when Joseph and Elsa expanded the farming operation with the purchase of the adjoining 120 acres. This transaction increased their homestead to two-hundred acres. The original log house was enlarged with the addition of a kitchen, porch, and second story for more sleeping room.

The living room and kitchen both measured eighteen feet by eighteen feet. A long wooden bench was conveniently placed near the door, a perfect spot to sit down and rest weary legs. On the nearby wall were hooks for hanging coats.

The kitchen table seated eight. A colorful oilcloth protected the warm oak finish. As in Finnish dining etiquette, the men and guests always ate first, children second, and the women last. The first cook stove was small with the ashpit on the side. Soon, it was replaced by a larger one with a warming closet and water reservoir. In the meantime, the smaller stove was moved into the summer kitchen for canning and general cooking on hot days. Both were fired by wood which was plentiful in the pastures. Twice daily, logs had to be chopped and carried into the woodbox from the shed outside.

Near the stove was a table for the water pails where dishes were washed. Also, the table was a convenient food prep station. A cupboard with two glass doors on top, two drawers below, and enclosed bottom shelves stored all the dishes, silverware and glassware.

Later on, Joseph bought a six-foot mirrored sideboard which was the forerunner to the buffet. Most of the wooden furniture was handmade by Finnish craftsmen. The folding davenport with a high back could be pulled out for sleeping similar to a daybed. The mattress was made of feathers with the cover and pillows sewn from red-and-white-checkered fabric. A kerosene lamp sat on top the large library table.

As the family size grew, additional furniture was needed. Joseph ordered a green velvet sofa from Sears Roebuck, that opened up for sleeping. Two leather Morris chairs flanked the sofa. Bars and notches in the back of the chairs made it possible to lower the cushion to reveal a twin bed. When overnight guests occupied a bedroom, the children were delegated to sleep in the chairs.

The master bedroom was on the main floor without a closet; instead clothing was hung from hooks or placed in dressers. Elsa and Joseph's bed frame was made of pine, and the treadle sewing machine was conveniently located in the corner of the bedroom. When Elsa had a spare moment, she sewed clothes for her children.

The other partitioned room near the kitchen was used as a food and dairy pantry instead of a bedroom. The floor had a trapdoor which led to the cellar. An opening between the floor was filled with sawdust for insulation. The discreet location served as a perfect hiding place for money because extra cash and coins were not always deposited in a bank.

A huge Boston fern hung by a chain from the ceiling, while family photographs and knickknacks rested upon the many shelves in the house. The kitchen walls were covered by wainscoting on the bottom and oilcloth on the upper half. Many of the local stores gave free calendars as Christmas gifts, some very elaborate. They became the art that graced the walls of the home.

The ceilings were made from rough-sawn lumber with grooves which were difficult to clean. The hardwood floors showed every spot of dirt and needed to be scrubbed often with a stiff brush and soap. Cleanliness was next to godliness, so the house was kept tidy most of the time.

The stately oak rocking chair stood in the kitchen parlor. Long rockers made the base of the chair sturdy, so it never tipped. Once children were born and old enough to walk, they'd climb up into Joseph's lap in the evening. Yawning from a long day's work, he rocked the little ones to sleep while humming the Finnish lullaby "Pium Paum Paukkaa," a song of rabbits running through the woods to bring berries to the child.

The bedroom and living room walls were covered with wallpaper in muted tones. Simple window treatments were roller shades and white lace curtains. They needed to be handwashed often to remove a buildup of black soot from the woodstove. Curtain stretchers were used to dry the lace and force them back into shape.

A homemade carpet covered the entire living room floor. Woven into two sections, the heavy rug separated for easier cleaning. Blue-

and-red stripes were intertwined so the colors lined up perfectly with the solid yellow background. During the summer, it was washed with a soapy brush, then rinsed in the river by the rapids. The rocks and fast-flowing current worked like an agitator pounding the dirt from the heavy rug.

The washbasin, alongside Elsa's homemade soap, was on top of a table in the kitchen. A roller towel for drying hands was fastened to the wall. The garbage pail rested under the stand.

Elsa said jokingly, "Seems like the woodbox was always empty and the garbage pail was always full."

CHAPTER 3

The Promised Land

And behold, the Lord stood above it and said, "I am the Lord,
the God of your father Abraham, and the God of Isaac; the land
on which you stand I will give to you and to your descendants."
—Gen. 28:13 (NASB)

CHILDREN FILLED THE HOUSE WITH laughter and merriment. Elsa
was "with child" when the couple moved to the homestead. Anna
was born in December of 1885. The sauna was used as the birthing
center, perhaps because it was considered sanitary. A local midwife
assisted in the delivery of Anna.

Kate followed and Maria arrived less than fifteen months later.
From the moment she could talk, precocious and beautiful Maria
preached salvation to anyone who would listen. Perhaps she sensed
an urgency to share with innocence the gospel as the little evangelist
died from whooping cough at the age of five. Ida was born shortly
after Maria's passing, and a grieving mother, Elsa found comfort
holding the baby close to her breast.

Finally after four daughters, Elsa gave birth to a son who was
named Henry after Joseph's father. Three years later, tragedy struck
once again when the boy died from measles. Joseph was heartbroken to lose his firstborn son. However, a year later, in 1894, Andrew
Edwin, Lynn's grandfather, was born and survived. Naturally, Joseph

bonded to Ed. The two remained devoted to each other until Joseph's death in 1946.

Twins Joe and Hjalmer were born in 1896. The two boys were inseparable, and as a result, Ed took them both under his "big brother's wing." Lydia, Selma, Henry, and Mamie followed in the birth order, completing the first family.

Joseph often said his children were the greatest gifts God gave him. Little did he know his seed would multiply, and hundreds of his offspring would disperse throughout the United States.

The family outgrew the original house, that was eventually remodeled in 1909. The stairway was relocated away from the kitchen. The roof was raised, and part of the front porch was enclosed where the new staircase was built, thus gaining access to the second floor. A windowed hallway led to two bedrooms, one for the boys and the other for the girls, as well as to an unfinished cold storage room.

Inside the boys' bedroom were two beds and another collapsible bed which could be folded up and put away to create more space. Inside the clothes closet was a box for leather. Young Ed made a table and two matching chairs for the room. The only heat available to the boys' bedroom was from a small opening chiseled in the chimney.

The girls' room was located directly above the living room. A floor register allowed heat to rise from the main level into the girls' bedroom. Two double beds were shared by the five sisters. A narrow closet along the edge of the outer wall held their frocks. The girls took turns inscribing special events on the closet door.

"Kate, Kate, will you measure to see how much I've grown?" begged Lydia, who wondered if she'd ever be as tall as her older sister.

Each room was papered, and the floors were painted and protected with runners made from tattered clothes. Thick wide logs were exposed in the unfinished room. Two additional beds, clothing, and extra groceries were stored there and preserved in the cold attic.

The first wood heaters were cast-iron with a tin upper plate to radiate more heat. Later, Joseph upgraded to a coal stove with a new feature the children called "icing glass." Much to their delight, the flames could be seen burning brightly within the chamber.

Often, Joseph heard his youngest child make requests. "Father, please make a fire in the stove so we can watch the flames wiggle back and forth," pleaded five-year-old Mamie.

"*Pikku tytto*," (little girl) Joseph gently reminded his youngest daughter, "it's midsummer, and the only fire I will make is a sauna fire for you to wash your dirty little toes."

During warmer months, the house was kept cooler by cooking in the "summer kitchen" adjacent to the main kitchen. Beneath it, a shallow well was eventually dug and a hand pump installed so that water was easily accessible in both summer and winter.

Porches surrounded both ends of the house. Along the north-side porch was a walkway and railing leading to the cellar entrance. A four-sided shed above the cellar secured its entrance while the stone foundation and dirt floor kept the root vegetables and meats preserved.

The original barn was north of the house and soon was too small for the family's needs. As a result, a log addition was built which was large enough for twenty head of cattle. The stalls were made of rough-sawn wood. Once the cow entered the barn, she ambled over to her stall, dipped her head to eat the hay in the trough. Then the farmer quickly slipped a chain around its neck tethering the animal, readied for milking.

According to Finnish custom, women milked the cows. Consequently, Joseph never mastered pulling teats. He managed to keep busy, though, with the countless other chores on the farm which included shoveling manure, something the girls preferred not to do.

For a time, finding quality livestock to buy was difficult. Then, one day, Joseph heard of two men who were selling a train carload of Guernseys. Quickly, he sought them out at the railroad yard and bought two cows. Next, he went to Cokato to buy a team of work horses. He had them shipped by train from Minneapolis to Thomson near Carlton, the county seat. From Thomson, he walked them four miles back to the homestead.

A hay shed was attached to the barn which held two large bins, one for middling and the other for bran. First, the hay was cut with a scythe, raked by hand into haycocks, and hauled to nearby sheds using two long poles. A hayfork and slings were used to transfer the hay into the sheds.

Timber became the first "cash crop" in the area. Seeing an opportunity, Joseph cleared more of his acreage, floating the logs down the Midway River to the Village of Thomson where there was a sawmill. He sold the timber and planted more hay in the fields. A McCormick mower and horse-drawn rake were purchased to speed up the process. The hay was pitched on a sled and hauled away to one of six sheds for storage until it was sold.

Behind the hay shed was the pigpen. Hogs were raised from early spring until fall butchering. The pork was cured and later eaten during winter months. The horses were kept separate from the cows in a stable that was across the road. The stable also had its own hayloft. Ed was delegated to care for the horses and, once a day, would cross the road to feed them. Joseph taught his eldest son, Ed, the art of horsemanship. He, in turn, handed that gift down to his son Raymond.

A carriage house stood near the northwest corner of the farm. Inside was a two-seated buggy with black leather upholstery and the cutter, a sleigh, having one long seat with a high curved front and red velvet cushions. A two-seated wagon and farm machinery were also stored in the carriage house. The wood shed was on the side of the building. Once in a while, it became the place for disciplinary action. Elsa left spankings to her husband. She was more apt to use flattery and compliments. Wise Elsa used this technique quite effectively on her husband, as well as her offspring.

There was always an ample supply of dry wood in the woodshed. Joseph preferred to split the majority of the logs on winter mornings, as it was much easier to do when frozen. Elsa said, "If there wasn't plenty of dry wood stored in the woodshed, it was a sign of a "shiftless husband." In fact, wood was used not only for heating the farmhouse but also for cooking, baking, heating water for the laundry, and for washing up.

The two-seat privy was just behind the carriage house. The outhouse was cold in the winter and stunk in the summer, even though lime was thrown down the holes. Wallpaper decorated the walls and old mail-order catalogues were used for toilet paper. A chamber pot conveniently placed in the upstairs hallway of the house was used during the night "when nature called."

The first smoke sauna was built below the hill closer to the river with easy access to water. Later, the small structure was moved near the house once a well was hand dug close by. A pulley with a long rope lowered the bucket down the well and fresh, cold, water was lifted to the surface. Instead of trudging down to the river with pail in hand, all one needed was a strong arm to pull up the bucket tied to the rope.

A smoke sauna did not have a chimney. The huge woodstove had an iron frame that was covered with stones fetched from the riverbed. A fire was built in the afternoon. Wood was added hourly until the rocks were hot by evening. The smoke was thick inside the sauna. The only way for it to escape was through a small opening in the ceiling. In order to add wood to the stove, you had to crouch down near the floor and hold your breath. Water was thrown onto the hot stones to get rid of the gas and smoke. Then the opening was closed. The rocks stayed hot all evening, and everyone had the chance to sauna.

Women and young children bathed first before the heat intensified. The sauna ritual lifted the inhibitions of the stoic Finnish people, and became a place where conversation spilled over. Two benches at different levels were designed to sit on while taking steam. Men sat on these benches for hours visiting freely, laughing and sharing stories. Then for added stimulation of the skin, a cluster of fragrant cedar or birch branches were tied together and used to slap oneself on the arms and shoulders.

The same soap Elsa made from the lard and glycerin was used to shampoo hair, wash bodies, and launder the clothes. Occasionally, the sauna was used to smoke meat, and a favorite treat after sauna was the dried beef.

Farther south from the sauna was another log building, the "*riihi*," used for drying grain. A rock stove heated the grain which was drying on high shelves. The hand-tied shocks were pounded against the wall and flayed on the floor with two poles connected to leather thongs. A large fan mill cleaned the kernels. The rye was threshed this way to save the straw, that was sold to Marshall Wells in Duluth where it was used to stuff horse collars.

Before the turn of the century, Joseph, together with sixteen area farmers, bought a steam threshing machine. During harvest time, a threshing crew led by John Sunnarborg, arrived at various farms and worked all day. The grain was put in large stacks in the *riihii* to dry. Later in the day, women prepared huge meals of meat and potatoes to feed the crew. Neighbor helped neighbor in the small township.

When a death occurred, *riihis* were often used to lay the body before burial. There was no embalming to preserve a body. Instead, the body was washed and fitted with fresh clothing. Shortly thereafter, the corpse in a hand hewn wooden casket was transferred to the parlor in the house for a one-day visitation and funeral.

Elsa was the first to pass away in 1924 at the age of sixty-three. Often, she complained of headaches. The practice of bloodletting was performed in the sauna but was unsuccessful in treating her head pain. The Pykkonen medical history revealed that several family members died of cerebral hemorrhages. That may have been the case for Elsa, as well, but autopsies were usually not performed.

Patriarch Joseph never remarried and remained on his beloved homestead until death. Yet well before his passing, his son, Ed inherited Meadowbrook Dairy. The firstborn male assumed ownership of the family farm; the aging parent remained on the premises under the care of the family until the end of his life.

Therefore, since widowed Joseph continued to live with Ed and Esther for another seventeen years, he was an integral part of their family and imparted Finnish traditions and wisdom to the children. When the new brick house was built, the drawing plans included a small bedroom on the main floor specially designated for Joseph.

Christianity was an important element of Joseph's life, and he faithfully attended Finnish church services. Most certainly, he and Elsa prayed for divine guidance throughout their lives and were blessed. The old man professed the strict Laestadian doctrine which included confession, forgiveness, and absolution. "Worldliness," following the ways of the world, was discouraged; and believers frowned upon alcohol consumption and dancing.

Still, before retiring for the night, Joseph took a swig from the blackberry brandy bottle hidden within his wardrobe closet. And if the radio, which he vehemently claimed was sinful, aired a lively song, his grandchildren noticed his foot tapping underneath the table.

Joseph spoke very little English, and anyone who wanted to converse with him had to speak Finnish. Consequently, his grandchildren became bilingual out of necessity.

Joseph and Ed, along with Ed's brother Henry, began delivering milk to the Cloquet area in 1919, first to grocery stores and later to homes. It was customary to create a name for farms who sold milk to the public. For this reason, Ed's sisters, Mamie and Selma, came up with the name Meadowbrook Dairy, signifying its geographical location near water and a meadow. The name remained for well over one hundred years.

Selling milk was the main source of income for the Juntunen family. Yet Ed and Henry had the foresight to market vegetables particularly potatoes. Often, the children could be seen in the fields picking rocks or picking potatoes. Much of the produce was marketed in Duluth, and the profits used to expand the dairy business.

Always on the lookout for quality livestock, Ed bought more cows, increasing the dairy herd of mostly Holsteins to fifty-two, keeping a few Guernseys. Their milk made the richest cream, and almost everybody preferred cream and butter in the days before low-fat, no fat. Milk was sold in local grocery stores and delivered to homes in Cloquet, Esko, and the surrounding area. In the beginning, summer deliveries were made by automobile. When roads became impassable in the winter, the horse-drawn sleigh was used, and a small kerosene stove kept milk from freezing. Daily milk production was about 145 quarts.

Following the end of World War II, scandal forced Henry to leave farming and move his wife and sons to Cloquet. Two young girls, taking a stroll through a wooded area near Harney, discovered wife Sylvia and a local man in a compromising position. Horrified, the girls darted home to tell their parents. Soon, word of the philandering couple spread like wildfire. Henry was devastated, and his teenage son became the brunt of jokes at the high school.

Henry sought counsel from his older brother Ed. As always, Ed took care of his family. He bought out his brother's interest in Meadowbrook Dairy and also purchased Henry's house across the road. Henry used the money to buy a small business and a two-bedroom bungalow in Cloquet. He honored his marital vows and remained with Sylvia. Later on, he became the proprietor of the first bowling alley in the wood town.

With Henry now out of the picture, a partnership between Ed and his sons was formally established, and additional housing nearby became available. Howard and wife, Inga, who were currently living at the farm, moved into Henry's two-story white clapboard house. A long front porch faced the road, and stately elm trees lined both sides of the driveway.

About the same time, the nearby Lahti Farm was for sale. The partnership of Ed Juntunen & Sons quickly acquired another huge barn for storage, forty acres, and a two-story house. Wally and his new wife, Donna, lived in the farmhouse for several years until they built a home directly across from Meadowbrook's barn. Then Willy took a turn living at the Lahti farm with his bride, Kathy.

Once again, Ed devised a perfect solution for everyone. He possessed godly wisdom beyond his years, a clear vision for the future, and the ability to resolve challenges.

Seems like Ed Juntunen always knew how to make lemonade from lemons. His sons looked to their father for direction and leadership. He lived by the Ten Commandments and honored Sundays. The only work permitted was the twice daily milking of the cows.

"The boys" disagreed with their father's insistence that no additional chores be done on the Sabbath. Despite these objections, they refrained from haymaking, plowing or the like on any given Sunday and by doing so observed the fourth commandment...honor thy father.

CHAPTER 4

The Heart of the Home

Children are a heritage from the Lord, The
‧ fruit of the womb is a reward.
—Psalm 127:3 (NKJV)

He who finds a wife finds a good thing
and obtains favor from the Lord.
—Proverbs 18:22 (NKJV)

ESTHER JUNTUNEN KNEW ALL ABOUT pregnancies, labor, and babies. She had given birth to sixteen children. In all, she was pregnant for over four thousand three hundred days. The babies were born at the house with the assistance of a midwife. No cervical block or epidural was available to alleviate labor pain. Instead, Esther endured hours of excruciating contractions.

Most farming families wanted many sons and daughters to help with the chores. That was true for Ed and Esther. Unfortunately, the pregnancies took their toll on the young woman. Two of the children, Leslie and Warren, died in infancy.

For most of her adult life, Mrs. Ed Juntunen Sr. was sickly. She was plagued with high blood pressure, heart disease, arthritis, and most likely fibromyalgia, which wasn't yet recognized as a medical condition. With her body aching most of the time, she spent many days sitting in a chair by the dining room window. She enjoyed looking outside watching the daily activities unfold, waiting for the milk trucks to return, worrying when they were late.

Esther was especially afraid of thunderstorms having twice witnessed lightning strikes. Once as a young woman, while Esther was washing clothes, lightning struck the washing machine. She had difficulty prying her hands from the metal washtub. Then several years later, a bolt hit the house chimney while her sons slept upstairs. With great force, the lightning jolted Raymond right out of his bed and unto the floor. A little dazed, young Ray crawled back up onto the small cot next to the chimney and soon fell asleep. After all, he had to get up for milking in a few short hours.

Understandably, these two episodes left Esther extremely anxious when dark clouds threatened the skies. Often, when there was a thunderstorm, her heart palpitated out of control. Not always sure what to do, Pa enlisted the help of his daughters, who were able to calm their mother's panic attacks by singing songs. Even though at the time, it was very much a "man's world," Ed relied heavily on the women of the family to comfort Esther. His heart was softest toward youngest daughter Barbara, who made a point every night to call down from the top of the staircase, "Good night, Mother. Good night, Father." Much like the closing scene from the TV series "The Waltons," filmed in the 1960s, it actually happened at Ed and Esther Juntunen's during the 1940s.

Esther's parents, Hugo and Sophie Sjoblad, first lived two miles west of the Juntunen homestead on Harney Road. Esther was the oldest of the seven daughters, who included Hilda, Olga, Helen, Violet, Jean, and Eleanor. The last child to arrive, much to Hugo's delight, was a baby boy. He was named Norman, and was only a few months older than his nephew Ray.

The Sjoblad family was musical and gregarious. Unfortunately, once Esther married Ed, she became more subdued, especially when her husband was nearby. The church culture encompassed strict teaching, and "do's and don'ts" stifled a woman, especially if she was an extrovert. Back in the day, a lady was discouraged from being outgoing or speaking her mind.

However, when her husband was out working on the farm or running errands in town, Esther was in charge. Her daughters cooked and cleaned all the while singing or dancing around the rooms. Laughter and merriment made chores appear to become a lighter load.

Three hot meals were prepared every day. Very early in the morning, a large pot of oatmeal bubbled on the stove. Heaping spoonfuls of sugar and large chunks of butter topped the bowls of "*boodua*" that the family ate in shifts. Shortly after the oatmeal pot emptied, noon-meal preparations began. Meat and potatoes were cooked every day. Beef, pork, and chicken were the choice meat selections, and on Saturdays, six pies were baked for the more elaborate Sunday dinner. Soon after that meal, dessert was served. The pies were carefully cut into eight slices and topped with a generous dollop of freshly whipped cream. Often, Raymond negotiated a deal with one of his brothers and bought their piece of pie for five cents. Both seller and buyer were pleased with the transaction.

One day for dinner, fresh garden peas were served. Since all the children were encouraged to eat their vegetables, four-year old Willy was asked to sample a few peas. Slyly he rolled several from his plate onto the floor, then shoved one way up his nose. Ed tried in vain to dig the pea from his son's nostril. The other children watched with amusement as their little brother screamed. After several failed attempts, Ed took Willy to the doctor's office in Cloquet. While Ed tightly held his son, the doctor removed the pea. For his bravery, the nurse rewarded Willy with a red lollipop. When father and son returned home, Willy found another pea on the floor and hastily pushed it up his nose, hoping to repeat a trip to the doctor. However, Ed wisely watched how the skilled physician removed the first pea and he was able to extract the second with the help of his wife. Consequently, the boy wasn't lickin' another lollipop; instead he got a lickin' from his pop.

People were always made to feel welcomed at the Juntunen home. Hospitality was a gift passed on from generation to generation. Before guests walked through the door, children scurried to pick up coffee cups from the kitchen table and flip the scatter rugs to their clean side. Then they quickly disappeared.

Pulla, a cardamon coffee bread, was saved for the visitors to devour. Butter and raspberry jam topped the delicious sweet bread served along with steaming cups of rich dark coffee.

Esther's daughters helped with housework, while her sons worked on the farm. Sometimes, there was a variation, and Dottie admitted that occasionally she milked the cows. Old Finnish tradition always had "the maids a-milking," but it was rare that any daughter of Ed's pulled teats. There was a time of exception when extra help was needed. During the war, three sons were overseas fighting the Nazis and Japanese.

Allen, Willard, and Wally served their country during World War II. Wilbur was stationed in Korea during that conflict. Their mother faithfully wrote letters to her sons every single day. Journaling became a part of her prayer life and the way she coped with fears for their safety.

She knew that every day they could possibly be in harm's way yet needed somehow to stay connected with the world they knew back in Esko. Every evening, she picked up her best pen and stationery to compose a letter about how much hay was baled that day or if Pa bought a new cow or if the milk trucks got stuck in the snow… just the everyday happenings at the dairy. Letter writing was therapy for Esther and was well received by her sons overseas.

Meanwhile, Ed knew good quality from livestock to furniture to clothing. He had an eye for the finest. This was especially true when it came to clothing. He would take Esther to an apparel store where he sat in a chair while Esther tried on dresses and matching hats. He nodded his head either in approval or disapproval when Esther stepped out from the dressing room. Not to be outdone, Ed bought his suits from a fine men's clothing store in Duluth owned by a Finnish man. It was customary for local Finnish businesses to patronize one another.

As the children grew older, additional living space was required. A new residence made of brick and tile was built in 1934 that replaced the original farmhouse. Never wasting good lumber, the shell from the first house was used to build a garage.

The new dwelling became the largest single family home in the township having seven bedrooms, three bathrooms, a formal dining room, living room with brick fireplace, spacious kitchen, walk-in pantry, and breakfast nook. The basement was equipped with a laundry room and, of course, a traditional steam sauna.

Even though new furnishings for the house were purchased, the pendulum clock from the first house was given a place of distinction. The timepiece ticked away on a walnut shelf behind Grandfather's rocking chair. Every Sunday Ed inserted the crank into the clock's two winding parts turning thirteen revolutions. On the Sunday when his heart stopped ticking, the clock stopped ticking, too.

While Esther's health deteriorated and her daughters left the nest, a local woman, Ellen, was hired to help with the laundry and ironing. For several days, she'd stand beside the ironing board and painstakingly press the wrinkles from Esther's cotton housedresses and the men's dress shirts and trousers. Since Ed was very particular about his wardrobe, Esther oversaw Ellen's duties. As a result, the man of the house was well-groomed and dressed in a tailored suit and a starched, white shirt with matching tie when he left for Sunday church services.

Also, over the years, Ed hired Finnish women to help, by preparing meals and with general housekeeping. In fact, a live-in maid worked at the house until Ed passed away in 1977. Lynn's favorite housekeeper was Jenny "*Yenny*" Kumpula. A widow with few relatives, Jenny became part of the Juntunen family. She was a kind, gentle soul, who only spoke and understood the Finnish language.

Before Jenny began her day in the Juntunen household, a few of "the boys," Raymond, Howard, Willy, Edwin, and Wally waltzed into the brick house to touch base with their Pa and make a plan for that particular day. They sat at the large kitchen table in the windowed alcove slurping hot coffee from saucers. Being impatient to wait for the coffee to cool, they poured small amounts from the cup to a saucer, picked up the saucer with both hands, and lifted it to the mouth.

In between a few words, slurp went the dark liquid to the lips. One very early morning sleepy Wally dozed off as he attempted to drink coffee from his saucer. His head bobbed twice before it slowly hit the table. Bam!

"Hey, Chester, (Wally's birth name) wake up! Time to go to work!" snickered brother Ray. About the same time, Jenny, made her entrance into the kitchen. Ed's sons found great enjoyment teasing sweet Jenny, who giggled and motioned with her right hand to stop their playful ribbing. Teasing aside, they were grateful for the housekeeper, who kept a watchful eye on their father and his big brick house. But resumed the merriment and howled when they heard Ed give directions to his place.

Since Finnish letters b and p, when spoken, sound similar, words might get misinterpreted. On occasion, Ray and his brothers overheard their dad explain that he lived in the "pig, prick house" on the Juntunen Road.

Chapter 5

Hit Head On By Grace

My grace is sufficient for you, for my power
is made perfect in weakness.
—II Corinthians 12:9 (NIV)

HIGHWAY 35 APPEARED TO BE *a bit slippery that eighth day of February,*
so Lynn proceeded carefully. She glanced at the clock on the dash. There
was plenty of time to get to her meeting place. She'd have an opportunity
to order a cup of coffee at the Hole in the Wall Café and catch her breath
before the women arrived at three o'clock.

Traffic was light, and the roads held a dusting of newly fallen snow.
Without warning, a dirty gray Chevy Blazer came from out of nowhere,
rounded the bend, and crossed over the median.

The driver of the Blazer, Grace, attempted to slam on the brakes. It
was a futile attempt. Two children, nine and fourteen years old, screamed
in the rear seats. They flopped from side to side in the back of the SUV.
Their seat belts were not fastened and their mother felt helpless as her
vehicle skidded into the front of Lynn's van.

The windshield shattered as the Blazer's reinforced bumper ripped
into the front of the van...the impact so great it pushed the engine into
the steering wheel. Both vehicles rocked together and screeched to a halt.

Lynn's van was hit head-on; she was hit head-on by Grace.

Two people saw the accident as it happened. Tim and Wendy
quickly pulled their vehicles over and stopped to see what they could do

to help. Another car slowly drove around the wreckage, and the driver yelled out, "I'll call 911."

The young woman came up to the smashed side window. She found Lynn pinned between the van's dash and front seat. She saw boxes and paperwork strewn everywhere and recognized an Avon brochure. Wendy's grandmother sold Avon products in Superior and was one of the district's most successful representatives.

Shortly thereafter, Tim from Brule, Wisconsin, rushed over to hear Lynn speaking hoarsely to him, "I think I'm dying... Tell my girls that I love them."

You see, when someone believes they are dying, what do they want to do? They want to leave final parting words for their loved ones. Lynn believed she was dying. Her spirit sensed that she was dying. What does a mother want to do when she believes her life was coming to an end?

"Tell my girls that I love them," mumbled Lynn to this stranger Tim, who just happened to witness the accident and stopped.

Less than five minutes passed before a Wisconsin Highway patrolman arrived. After quickly looking over the situation, he radioed for assistance.

The Life Flight helicopter from St. Mary's Hospital determined that poor visibility made it impossible to land on the snowy surface of Highway 35.

"We're going to need three ambulances to Highway 35 just north of Danbury ASAP," he spoke to the dispatcher. "We have a female trapped in a van and another woman with two kids in a Chevy Blazer. Looks like it was a head-on."

"Ambulances are en route and should arrive in about fifteen minutes."

Meanwhile, Wendy stayed and comforted Lynn, who remained awake and responsive. Tim walked over to the other vehicle to check on the children and their mother. They were rattled, but their injuries appeared to be non-life-threatening.

Township volunteer responders arrived first. Another squad car and three ambulances followed. Four people needed to be taken to Duluth hospitals thirty miles away.

The first responders assessed Lynn and quickly concluded that she needed immediate attention. The driver's side door would not open; the van's rear door was jimmied open with a crow bar. The jaws of life pried the backseat out from the frame of the vehicle in order to get to the front seat. A cable was attached to the bucket seat where Lynn was pinned, and very slowly and carefully, it was pulled away from the steering wheel.

After ninety minutes of painstakingly dismantling the minivan, the rescue team extricated Lynn from the mangled heap. She was placed on a stretcher and carried to the waiting ambulance. By then, Grace and her children were already at the emergency room being treated for their injuries.

The patrolman searched the vehicle and found Lynn's wallet with identification. He radioed the information to St. Mary's. Then a staff woman from the triage team called the Davidson home.

Unsuspecting, Brooke, a senior in high school, answered the call.

"Is this the Davidson household where Lynn Davidson lives?" the caller asked.

"Yes, it is," replied Brooke.

"May I ask what is your relationship to Lynn?" the nurse continued.

Brooke answered, "I'm her daughter."

"Is your dad at home?"

"No, can I take a message?" Brooke asked.

"I'm sorry to have to tell you that Lynn has been in an accident and is being taken by ambulance to St. Mary's Hospital in Duluth," she continued.

Stunned, Brooke hung up the phone and rushed to the school to get her father, who at the time was refereeing a junior high basketball game. Taken aback, Russ darted out of the gym to the car where daughter Amy sat in shock. The three went back to the house and called daughter Robyn, who was living and working in the Twin Cities. Then Russ called Janet, and asked if she and Danny could take them to the hospital. He was too upset to drive. Also, Brooke called Grandma Jackie, while Russ changed from his striped ref shirt to a new blue pullover that his wife had bought only days before.

Lynn's sister, and brother-in-law, arrived at the house to get Brooke, Amy, and Russ. During the twenty-minute ride to Duluth, no one said a word. All of them were deep in thought wondering, would Lynn be alive?

CHAPTER 6

Born for a Purpose

Before I formed you in the womb I knew you, before you were
born I set you apart and appointed you for a special purpose.
—Jeremiah 1:5 (AMPC)

WE ARE BORN INTO THIS world for a purpose greater than ourselves.
We need to discover that purpose in order to fulfill God's plan for
our lives.

The Ed Juntunen family grew, and life was good. All of the
children married except the youngest son, Tommy. He was born with
muscular dystrophy. Although doctors determined Tommy to have
a life expectancy of only eighteen years, he defied all odds and lived
until at thirty-one his heart gave its last beat. Ed discovered him lying
peacefully on the kitchen floor and, three days later, buried him at
the church cemetery next to Esther.

Yet where there is death, there is also new life. Every year during
the fifties and sixties, a grandchild or two was born. The year 1952
was no exception, as a baby girl was about to leave the protection of
her mother's womb.

The September morn dawned cool and crisp. Mildred began the
day much like a typical Monday by going into the basement to do
laundry. She separated the whites from the colored clothes and tossed
the first load into the conventional washing machine. Meanwhile,
upstairs, both children were getting ready for school. Classes had

been in progress for three weeks for Janet in second grade, while Rodney was a fifth grader.

Mildred hurried up the basement steps and felt a slight cramp in her lower abdomen. She didn't have time to dwell on the pangs. Soon the school bus would be coming. Janet and Rodney needed to have breakfast, brush teeth, and get out to the end of the driveway. Mildred did not want her children to be late for Eino Ikola's bus. She prided herself in being punctual, and that was a trait she wanted her children to learn as well.

After seeing the kids safely on the bus, Mildred continued her daily routine. The slight pain in her groin continued, but she was determined to get the laundry done. She carried the heavy clothes basket up the basement steps and out to the clothesline in the back-yard. The autumn sunshine and light westerly winds would quickly dry the towels and sheets. They would smell so fresh for tonight's bedtime. She wondered if Ray would notice.

Ray's senses were keener since he lost vision in his right eye. There was a silver lining in the cloud which took away his sight. He became ineligible for the armed service, unable to serve his country as a soldier in World War II. Many of his buddies, as well as three brothers, either enlisted or were drafted. The men were stationed overseas fighting the Germans or the Japanese. Half blind, Ray remained at home on American soil with his wife and young family.

Because of the war, there was a shortage of men working in the factories. Therefore, even with only one seeing eye, Ray was hired at the Diamond Match, a factory that made wood stick matches and toothpicks. He operated heavy equipment with the skill of any two-eyed laborer.

While Ray worked for ten years operating a crane in the wood-yard at the Diamond Match, he was sorely missed on the family farm. His father, Ed, wanted him back to help with an expansion. Ray honored his father's wishes and returned to longer hours, harder work, and no retirement pension.

As a token of appreciation for returning to Meadowbrook Dairy, Ed promised his son one acre of land on which to build a modest house. Workhorses were becoming obsolete. Their pasture across the road from the farmhouse became the site for Ray's new house. Construction was completed during the summer, and Ray moved his wife and two children into their three-bedroom rambler just before Thanksgiving of 1950.

There was much to be thankful for that year. The war was over, and Ray was back working on the family farm with his father and five brothers. His son Rodney and daughter Janet were healthy and happy. His wife was humming in the kitchen preparing a feast. Their new home was filled with laughter and the aroma of turkey and freshly baked pies. Yet something was missing.

Given that, fourteen months later, Mildred announced that she was with child. Also, during the same year, two of her sisters, Alice and Lola, and two sisters-in-law, Lorraine and Shirley, were pregnant. The baby boom of the '50s was booming. For Ray and Mildred, soon the anticipation would be over. A child was coming, another mouth to feed; Ray needed to get his wife to the hospital.

He changed from his dirty work pants and shirt into clean ones. Mildred did the laundry earlier that morning. She hobbled to the clothesline in the backyard. She took pleasure in being the first in the neighborhood to hang out Monday's wash. Yet, on this particular day, her swollen belly made this household task quite difficult. As she stretched her arms to reach the clothesline, her water broke and gushed between her legs into the grass.

Between contractions, Mildred tried to hurry her husband along. "Please, will you huuuurrry up!"

"Okay," he replied as he usually did to his wife's cajoling.

Still, Ray needed to wash the field grime from his youthful-looking face and rough, worn hands as best he could. Despite her pleas, Ray resumed his usual slow but sure pace. He was the turtle who married a hare.

As water flowed from the faucet, his thoughts flowed freely. He recalled that in the past his wife had labored long and hard. Mildred delivered their firstborn, a son, Rodney, ten years earlier, followed by a little girl, Janet Renee, three years after that. Seven years had passed, and Mildred was pregnant once again. Ray believed his wife would reach the hospital in plenty of time, so his mind continued to wander.

A bumper crop of potatoes was harvested this September. The musty root cellar below the toolshed held about 2,300 bushels. The crop would bring a handsome profit that would pay for seed potatoes next spring and a new plow. Eventually the mammoth work horses, Prince and Dan, would be phased out in 1958 by a new Flambeau red Case tractor.

Ray had grown fond of the Percherons and would be sad once the day came when they must be sold. After his father's visit, Ray's mouth gave a soft cluck to his four-legged friends and guided them from the potato field to the horse stable. Then he tethered Prince and Dan to their stalls, filled the hayrack and water pail, and walked home.

As it was, Mildred's water broke while she was hanging clothes in the backyard. Gingerly, she walked back to the house and just happened to see Inga on her steps next door.

Mildred hollered to neighbor Inga, "My water just broke underneath the clothesline! Will you call the farm so someone can tell Ray to come home?"

Inga, a registered nurse, knew her sister-in-law needed to get to the hospital and fast. She ran into the kitchen and called her mother-in-law. Esther answered the telephone, "Pa is just finishing his coffee. He'll go right away to the field to get Raymond."

Ray had a full schedule ahead. After the morning milking and Mildred's pancake breakfast, he picked up raw milk in twenty-gallon cans from fifteen farmers in the township. He trucked *maito* (milk) back to the milk house where Wally and Willard were waiting to process and bottle enough for the next day's deliveries. Then he greased the wheels on the trailer and prepared to go out to the field.

The day was shaping up for perfect conditions to dig potatoes before the ground froze and hardened. The cellar behind the barn was cool and dark, holding bushels of russets and red *pottus* (Finnish slang for potatoes). However, on this last Monday of September in 1952, an interruption occurred.

As Ray hunched down by the potato picker, Ed rounded the corner of the barn. Quickly, he walked out to the field toward his son. The Juntunen family had worked this land for over seventy years. Father Joseph taught his eldest son, Ed, the ways of successful farming. Both men passed those skills down to Raymond, who enjoyed working the earth and patiently waiting for the harvest.

Six of the sons were in partnership with their father. Even though they were adults, Pa usually referred to them as "the boys." This wasn't a put-down. While he was alive, the sons deferred to their father in business decisions. His wisdom was respected, and "the boys" counted on his leadership.

Time for milking was soon to begin, and Ray didn't notice his father come up from behind.

Startled, he asked his dad, "What? Are you coming to tell me you're gonna milk so I can stay in the field to pick more potatoes? We'll be able to sell many bushels and still have enough for us to eat all winter long."

"No, Ray, you better quit for the day. Inga called Ma to let you know that the baby is coming," Pa calmly said.

"Oh." Ray paused for a moment. "Okay, then, can you call Howard to come milk for me?" he asked.

"*Joo, joo,* (yes, yes), and if he can't, I will milk for you."

"Thanks, Pa," said the grateful son to his father. "I better get going home. Mildred will be in a hurry."

The workhorses rested early that day. Other duties were calling their handler, who, with long slow strides, walked home prepared to be hurried up by his anxious wife. Ray knew that he needed to get her to the hospital in Cloquet as soon as possible. The facility was only a ten-minute drive from Esko, but Mildred was in labor with their third child.

She called out again to her husband, "Ray!"

Quickly, he snapped back to reality, dried his hands on the towel, and grabbed Mildred's suitcase as she wobbled out the door and into the car.

Meanwhile, across the road at the farm, Pa lined up Howard to do the barn chores and milking. The brothers helped each other whenever possible. Howard was designated as the "spare man," and he could fill in for any of the boys. Willard and Wally processed and bottled the milk. Edwin and Willy delivered the milk along with cousin Gordy. Ray was the "barn boss," who milked and tended the cows. After barn chores, he worked the fields along with one of the nephews or a hired hand. Meadowbrook Dairy, Ed Juntunen & Sons, was a family-owned business, and the family was quietly very proud of its success.

Ray often commented, "All us boys get along and never seem to have any trouble agreeing on what's best for Meadowbrook."

If there was a disagreement, Pa had the final word. After all, he was the president of the partnership, Ed Juntunen & Sons. Occasionally, they joked about him behind his back. Yet they respected their father and recognized his wisdom and leadership.

Ed was wise enough to know that Mildred's third time in labor and delivery might be much quicker than the previous ones. Hadn't each successive one of Esther's sixteen birthing experiences been a little easier?

Well, maybe not, he thought. A woman endured much discomfort when delivering a child. New life was indeed a precious process...one of God's miracles. Ed knew that Mildred was a strong, tough woman, yet she needed a ride to the hospital and Raymond better get moving and fast!

While waiting for her husband, she phoned her mother, Fannie, and made arrangements for Rodney and Janet to be dropped off after school at the Sunnarborgs. Then she called her sister Lola, who, in turn, called Alice, who called sister-in-law Lorraine. Both Lola and Lorraine had given birth to sons that same year of 1952, and Alice was due to have her baby in a couple of weeks.

Ray's mother would contact his sisters and brothers once the baby arrived. Other friends and family members would be notified later.

As Ray drove five miles to the hospital in downtown Cloquet, he glanced over to his wife and wondered whether she would deliver a boy or a girl this third time. He was thankful for his little family and decided that, as long as the baby was healthy, that's all that mattered.

Lost in his thoughts, he recalled the many ways new life began daily on the farm. From potato shoots bursting forth from the fertile soil to a calf's wet head slipping out from a cow's loins. These were the moments of new birth.

Occasionally, Ray was called upon to give a helping hand. More than once, he plunged his strong arms into the laboring cow's backside, turning around a breach calf for safe entry through the birth canal. Most certainly, Ray understood new life and was about to experience it again, when the baby burst on the scene late that September eve.

Upon arriving at the Raiter Hospital, Mildred was whisked away to the maternity ward. Expectant fathers did not enter the delivery room to serve as coaches for their wives. Instead, they sat in a waiting room and smoked cigarettes.

Mindlessly, Raymond studied the pictures in the *Look* magazine but couldn't concentrate. He spotted a small table in the corner which was designated as a coffee station. A cup of the rich dark java along with a sugar cookie was just what he needed. Suddenly, a doctor triumphantly pushed open the swinging door. All eyes looked up.

Dr. Monserud stopped, looked at the men, and asked, "Who is Marge Anderson's husband?"

A nervous little man in the corner jumped up and shouted, "I am!"

"You have a son, Mr. Anderson."

The man looked dazed, attempting to process the good news, when his legs buckled and he collapsed to the floor.

The doctor yelled for the nurse, "Get the smelling salts."

But before she arrived with them, Mr. Anderson revived on his own.

Doc said, "Are you okay? No need to be embarrassed, Mr. Anderson. This happens all the time."

Sheepishly, the man got to his feet and asked, "When can I see Marge and the baby?"

"Soon," replied the doctor, "but, first, we are getting both the baby and your wife freshened up. A nurse will get you shortly."

Then the doctor quickly left the room. He knew Mildred was ready to bear down and would be next to deliver. He changed into fresh scrubs, washed his hands, and walked into the other delivery room.

"Are you ready to get this over with, Mrs. Juntunen?" he asked.

"I sure am," Mildred replied between huffs and puffs.

And in less than a half hour, the baby arrived. Once washed, toweled, and printed, the baby was brought back to her mother where the first moments of bonding occurred.

Meanwhile, Dr. Monserud made his way back to the waiting area. He halted in front of Ray and announced, "It's a girl…tiny, little thing, five pounds, two ounces but healthy and making a lot of noise already, Ray."

The doctor shook Ray's brawny hand, who sighed a bit from relief and grinned with gratitude that the wait was over.

An hour later, Mother smiled wearily as Ray entered Raiter's maternity wing. He was thankful Mildred at thirty-two hadn't had any complications throughout the pregnancy.

"I saw the baby down the hall in the nursery." He beamed. "She's so little. Her head isn't much bigger than an orange."

Tenderly, he kissed his wife and wondered aloud what they should name her.

Mildred said, "I like the name Lynn."

"Okay, so do I." He wasn't going to disagree with a woman who had just given birth.

Then Mildred added, "I think her middle name should be Rae after you but spelled r-a-e, instead of r-a-y."

"Yah." Ray smiled and agreed. "That would be nice."

So right then and there, it was decided. The baby girl was to be named Lynn Rae—*Lynn*, a Gaelic word meaning "stream or a lake" and *Rae* after her daddy.

Ray liked the sound of that and repeated it once again to his wife, "Lynn Rae."

This newborn was destined to become daddy's little girl, who loved the water.

Both infant and mother rested comfortably when Ray left the hospital. He drove home in the stillness of near dawn. Along the North Road, Ray noticed the harvest moon shining brightly across the pavement. The fifty cows in the night pasture were ready to be herded back to the barn for the morning milking. Their udders were already leaking of milk. Ray heard their gentle mooing as he stepped out from the Dodge sedan.

As the light of daybreak beckoned him to the milking parlor, Ray pondered his responsibility to his family, as well as to his cows. Both needed him for food, shelter, and protection. He accepted his role and, without complaint, faced the new day, another moment in life.

He made a promise to himself. He would do everything in his power to keep his daughter safe from harm. Little did he know that, forty-two years later, Lynn would be fighting for her very life.

CHAPTER 7

Fighting to Live

For great is your love toward me, you have
delivered me from the depths of the grave.
—Psalm 86:13 (NIV)

THE FAMILY WAS MET AT the hospital emergency room by the attending physician. He explained that a quick examination of Ms. Davidson had been made but the extent of Lynn's injuries was still being determined. There were several broken bones and a collapsed lung, and she was being assessed for internal injuries.

Russ was allowed to see his wife. Her cream-colored wool coat and matching boots had been sheared off. They lay on the chair in a neat pile. Not a scratch appeared on Lynn's face, yet her lower torso was badly broken. The tiny 4.5-size ring finger was beginning to swell from the intravenous fluids being pumped into the body. A nurse removed Lynn's wedding ring and gave it to Russ. With hands shaking, he slipped it into his pants pocket and later gave it to Brooke, wondering if his wife would ever wear it again.

Russ thought the small cubicle where Lynn lay was stuffy. Hospital staff continually asked Russ questions or wanted his signature on consent forms. He needed air and space, but it was not to be.

Lynn kept repeating to Russ the steps he needed to take in order to contact her company divisional manager, Kathye. "Call 1-800-555-1122, and tell them what happened," she expressed over and over to her husband. Although she lay half dead, she remained in a working mode. She wanted to clarify that the car accident had not been her fault. She feared her family would blame her in some way.

"There was nothing I could do. The car just came straight at me," she pleaded.

Russ soothed his wife, saying, "Yes, we know. It was not your fault."

After a brief visit from her sister and daughters, Lynn was taken into surgery to plate her arms and place screws in the knee and ankle to stabilize the broken bones.

The hospital chaplain, Joan Felling, walked with the family to the fourth-floor surgical waiting area. Bewildered, they sat and waited for the orthopedic surgeon to finish putting Lynn back together again.

Russ asked the chaplain, "Could you pray for my wife?"

"Of course," she replied. Then the family gathered around Chaplin Joan, and she called upon Almighty God to bring healing to Lynn and peace to her family.

While Robyn made her way up north, she tearfully gripped the steering wheel and cautiously drove the white Toyota Celica along slippery I-35 from Minneapolis to Duluth. Unlike today, cell phones were just becoming attainable. Most people did not own one. So for two hours, Robyn was not in contact with anyone. Silently and alone, she prayed too, wondering if she'd find her mother dead or alive.

Janet called her parent's clergyman, Rev. Ray Hilman from the Apostolic Lutheran Church. She asked the pastor if he would go to Mildred and Ray's and check on the couple. Besides hearing about the car accident, earlier in the day, Mildred learned that her youngest brother, Kenny, had been diagnosed with lung cancer. Two huge blows in one day were overwhelming to these senior citizens. Pastor Hilman offered to drive Mildred and Ray to the hospital. They accepted with gratitude his offer.

Waiting began in the waiting area. An army of people began showing up at the hospital to offer support. Russ's parents, Jackie and Ed, arrived, followed by Tom Pantsar, Lynn's godson. Finally, Robyn appeared after a long fearful drive from Roseville.

Onward, Christian soldiers were marching off to war. There was a war in the heavens, a battle between Lynn living or dying. The powerful army of prayer warriors was rocking the spiritual world. Prayer chains, groups of people who could be easily accessed by a phone tree, quickly heard of the accident and of Lynn's condition.

Although the communication speed of the Internet and the Caring Bridge website did not yet exist, news of Lynn's accident and her critical injuries rippled across the telephone lines. Intercessors from the East Coast to the West Coast fervently prayed for Lynn and her family. It was from their mouths to God's ears.

*****

"Lord, hear my voice; let your ears be attentive to the voice of my supplications" (Psalm 130:2)

Do we have the audacity to think we can change the course of a life by praying? Believe it or not, praying for someone to live, if they are close to death, is done every day by people around the world. On February 8, 1994, Lynn's family and friends did just that. They prayed and hoped her life would be spared.

Would she be granted a second chance? Could an Omnipotent God be swayed? Could praying prevent a death from cancer or a suicide? Or if an innocent bystander is abducted and never found, did prayers fail? Of course not!

Nobody has answers to those heart breaking questions "why me? why them?" They swirl around in our minds and frustrate us. At some point, to regain inner peace, we must accept not "my will", but "thy will be done." We must try to live with loss and death and heartache. No one is exempt. Eventually, everyone faces these challenges with their deep wrenching pain.

By placing the pain in God's hand, he will pull us toward his heart and give us strength to continue living. Will we dig deep asking God to help us in our time of distress?

Lynn's family and friends had the audacity to seek God and boldly pray that she wouldn't die. Prayer helped them cope with this crisis one moment at a time. They knew not the outcome, but every fiber of their being believed they must seek the One who created the little girl with crooked bangs.

So they prayed and prayed and prayed.

CHAPTER 8

Home for the First Time

A wife of noble character who can find? She is
worth more than rubies. Her husband has full
confidence in her and lacks nothing of value.
—Proverbs 31:10,11 (NIV)

A WEEK PASSED BEFORE MILDRED was sent home from the Raiter
Hospital with her healthy baby girl. Lynn's birth weight dropped to
under five pounds, still the doctor was not alarmed. The baby latched
onto her mother's breast, slurping milk. Mildred was a natural after
feeding two children before Lynn Rae.

Once home, mother and newborn settled in to a house filled
with well-wishers bearing gifts and food. A constant stream of family
and friends shuffled in and out. Seven-year-old sister Janet enjoyed
all of this excitement and wanted some attention too. After all, she
had been the little girl in the house, and now this baby girl had come
along. She planned a strategy and hoped it would work.

On Wednesday, just before 8:00 a.m., Janet quietly whispered
to her mother, "I don't feel good. My tummy hurts." Being a concerned mother, Mildred kept her daughter home from school. She
heard that the flu was going around ever since students were back
at school, coughing, sneezing, and exposing each other to all kinds
of viruses. Millie worried it might spread throughout the household. Janet never vomited but moped around until a visitor arrived

bearing gifts for the baby and sometimes for "big sister," too. Then she quickly sprang up and sat next to her mother while Mildred showed off the newborn. This pattern of tummy aches and absenteeism repeated itself for another day. Janet's second-grade teacher, Ruth Hendrickson, wondered why her student hadn't returned to the classroom and planned to meet with Mrs. Juntunen very soon.

The following Monday, parent-teacher conferences were held. Mildred drove to the Washington School to visit first with Rodney's fifth-grade teacher, then following up with Janet's teacher. It was Millie's first solo outing after giving birth. How good she felt to once again get behind the steering wheel and drive north along the Canosia Road. She passed by Sunnarborg Road where her parents lived and knew she could've left her children there while she visited with the teachers. Conveniently, Ray quickly volunteered to watch his three children, since he had no desire to attend parent-teacher conferences. Mildred wasn't too upset. Most fathers during the fifties opted out of these meetings.

She parked the car at her sister Alice's house which was located next to the elementary school and checked in with the Michaelsons. Alice was due any day with her third child. Babies were coming into the family at a steady pace, three more expected before the end of 1952.

Alice smiled when she saw her oldest sister come through the door and asked, "Are you here all by yourself?"

"Yes, Ray is with the kids," she replied and then asked, "Can I park in your driveway? The school's lot is full because of conferences."

"Sure," Alice answered.

"Would you want to walk with me to the school?" Mildred inquired.

"No, but thanks," was her reply. No way, thought Alice, was she going to conferences in her condition. The baby was due any day. Her feet were swollen and puffy. Besides, both her daughter and son were doing well by the looks of the corrected assignments they brought home.

"Okay, then, but I better get going. I don't want to leave Ray too long with all three kids." She snorted. "Not sure what he'd do if Lynn Rae poops in her diaper."

Both sisters laughed at the thought.

Then Mildred quickly left the Michaelson home and walked alone across the playground to the school. The cool night air felt refreshing. It seemed like ages since she'd walked briskly by herself.

The heavy front door swung open to the Washington School hallways, which overflowed with parents. Classrooms for grades four through six were up on the second floor. Mildred trudged up the wide wooden staircase and surprisingly was out of breath. She made a mental note to try to get back into shape. This third pregnancy and childbirth had taken its toll on her body. She reasoned, though, that she was only thirty-two years old, and housework would be exercise enough.

The second floor occupied the upper elementary grades. Mildred spied Mrs. Juntti's classroom and casually entered. Several parents were looking around the room at art and science projects made by the students for this evening's open house.

Mrs. Juntti spotted Mildred and called to her, "Come on over, and take a look at what your son did today in social studies."

Although Rodney was doing B work in grade five, he scored a perfect paper on the quiz, and both parent and teacher knew he was capable of doing better than average work. Yet the lad was maturing quickly. Along with his cousin David, Rodney enjoyed teasing girls obsessively. Mrs. Juntunen knew that the teasing gene had been inherited from both boys' fathers.

After the short visit with Mrs. Juntti, Mildred made her way down to the first floor to her daughter's classroom. She was interrupted by other women who wanted to congratulate her on the birth of the baby.

How gratifying, Mildred thought, it was to live in a small community and to know so many people who cared that she had recently brought home a newborn.

Janet's teacher cared about her second-grade students as well and was puzzled by Janet's absenteeism. That was until yesterday when she put two and two together. She concluded that, in her opinion, Janet wanted to stay home from school and be a part of all the festivities surrounding the birth of the baby. People dropped by with gifts and food. Janet would rather play house with her new "baby doll" than go to school.

Mildred thanked Mrs. Hendrickson for her keen observation and decided to wait until morning to talk to Janet about school truancy. She quickly left the building and did not stop again at her sister's. Instead, Millie slipped into the car and drove three miles to her house, glancing down at her gingham dress. Although she'd been away for only a couple of hours, her breasts were beginning to hurt and leak milk. Baby Lynn was due for another feeding, and so was her mom.

Ray sat comfortably in the rocker by the window. Sleeping in his arms was his baby girl. He still couldn't believe this child could be discharged from the hospital weighing under five pounds. Regardless, Dr. Monserud was confident the baby would be just fine. Mildred, after all, was an experienced mother, not only in regards to her own children but also for many others as well. Being eldest daughter in her family, she cared for and nurtured the younger Sunnarborg siblings. In fact, she remembered at sixteen coming from school only to discover a baby sister, Betsy was born. Mildred never knew her mother was pregnant! Fannie always wore loose fitting dresses, never revealing a baby bump. What a surprise to walk in the house after school and see her father John holding a tiny baby with a head of dark curls!

He boasted, "Come, see what we have here, Mildred!"

"What? Ma just had a baby?"

"Yo, yo! And isn't she a beauty!" Pa boasted and then ordered, "bring her to Ma. She's in the bedroom."

In shock Mildred obeyed her father and carried the newborn to the back bedroom. There she watched as Fannie lifted her nightgown and placed Betsy near her breast.

That was back in October of 1935. However, on this October eve, Mildred rushed from school conferences to feed her baby girl.

She hurriedly washed her hands in the kitchen sink and dashed to her husband. Without explanation she snatched the baby from Ray's burly arms and slid into the green club chair. As the child nestled into her mother's full breast and suckled contentedly, Mildred updated her husband on the teacher conferences.

The other two children were in their separate bedrooms tucked in for the night, yet not asleep. Listening carefully to their parents' muffled voices, both tried to understand the conversation in the living room but were unsuccessful. Hence, Rodney and Janet decided to snuggle down under their handmade quilts and close their sleepy eyes. Morning's light would come soon enough, and Mom's recap of their teachers' conversations could wait.

CHAPTER 9

Clip, Snip, Clip!

Even the very hairs of your head are numbered.
—Matthew 10:30 (NIV)

As THE LITTLE GIRL WENT from baby to toddler, her thin light-brown hair grew and bleached from sunshine mixed with river water. Waves formed at the nape, especially when the hair was slightly damp. The length never reached beyond Lynn's shoulders and never would.

Clearly, Millie, on a tight budget, wanted to keep her family neatly coiffed. At the time, pixie haircuts were fashionable and easy to maintain. So Mildred attempted to cut Lynn's hair into this new hairdo. Scissors appeared one afternoon, and Lynn was forced to sit still on the kitchen stool with an old bath towel draped around her shoulders.

"I don't want my hair cut," pleaded the little girl. "Why can't I have long hair so I can put it in a ponytail?"

"Your hair is thin and gets so dirty in the summertime. It's just easier to keep short."

In any case, the untrained hairstylist never quite mastered the art of cutting bangs without getting them crooked. Attempting to correct the unevenness only made matters worse. The little girl's bangs got shorter and shorter until the front hair was nearly cut to the scalp. Bystanders wondered if the little girl had tried to cut her own hair. Truth be told, it was "scissor-happy" Millie.

"Oh, your hair grows fast," was Mildred's explanation when her haircutting techniques were questioned.

Since there was no barber in Esko during the fifties, men went to neighboring towns for their haircuts. Ray worked long hours on the farm and rarely had an opportunity to visit a barbershop. Resourceful Millie found a solution to the dilemma.

One day, while shopping at the Ben Franklin store, she spotted a barber's kit with two shears, an electric clipper, cape, and two combs. Convincing herself that anyone can learn to give a decent haircut, she bought the kit. After supper that night, she carefully read the manual. When she finally got enough courage, she practiced the crew cut on her husband and son. To freshen up the flattops every ten days or so, the clippers were pulled out from the green box in the linen closet. After a while, Millie honed her barbering skills and wasn't all that bad.

She never did master cutting Lynn's stick straight bangs without getting them crooked. Fortunately, home permanents were introduced to the market. Two weeks before school started, girls were subjected to unusual cruelty. Throughout the United States, mothers purchased kits and attempted to curl their daughter's locks into tight frizzy ringlets.

Tonette home permanents were designed especially for the younger girls. First, the hair was tightly wrapped in rubber banded plastic rods. Then a pink solution that softened the hair follicle was applied to each rod. The strong odor wafted throughout the entire house. If any solvent dripped into the eyes, which always did, they painfully stung for several minutes.

Timing was critical for the perm to process accurately. The round white kitchen timer was set for thirty minutes. *Tick, tick, tick,* went the timer until the buzzer sounded "*ding.*" Then the rods were rinsed for five minutes, followed with a towel wrapped around the head for another fifteen minutes.

Next, the neutralizer, not as noxious as the first solution, was applied to each rod. Another thirty-minute wait ensued, ending with a cool water rinse for another five minutes. At that point, the "victim child" was totally waterlogged. Then the painful rod removal commenced.

"Ouch! Ouch! You're pulling out my hair," cried the little girl.

"No, you still have plenty, and it's curly," retorted the mother. Lastly, each hair strand was trimmed of the fishtail ends, the result of incorrect wrapping. *Clip, snip, clip.*

"Hooray! The back-to-school Tonette is all done," Mother cheered, "and as you now well know, girls have to suffer to be beautiful!"

Lame excuse, thought Lynn, for the torture she just endured for the past three hours.

Later on Saturdays, after sauna, Jenny, Grandpa Ed's maid, walked over to Raymontti's house to get her hair set. Mildred, the only daughter-in-law who spoke Finn, visited with Jenny while Lynn set her hair in pin curls. The young girl carefully parted the thin graying hair, then twirled each strand around her index finger. She crisscrossed two bobby pins, securing the curl.

After a hairnet and, *huivii,* (scarf) were tied around Jenny's head, she graciously thanked the little girl, "Kiitos paljon!"

Then she reached inside her front trouser pocket for a lace handkerchief and carefully opened it to reveal two quarters inside the white folds. She picked them up with her soft wrinkled fingers, well-worn from years of domestic work, and placed them into the girl's youthful palm. The coins were payment for the hairstyling services. Lynn tried to refuse, but the woman insisted. Although a widowed housekeeper, Jenny's pride remained intact, and she paid for the services rendered.

Those quarters were the first money Lynn earned for styling someone's hair. Just a few years later, she would attend beauty college, working ten years as a hairstylist. But the first of Lynn's customers was dear kind Jenny.

CHAPTER 10

Intensive Care

Though he slay me, yet I will hope in him.
—Job 13:15 (NIV)

MULTIPLE INJURIES AND TRAUMA TO *Lynn's body were life-threatening. Doctors were unsure if she'd survive the first night.*

Finally, about 7:00 p.m., an internist, Dr. Charlie Bertel, stopped by the family waiting area. All eyes were on him as he explained, "A tube was inserted into Lynn's right lung, and we were able to successfully reinflate it. Also, it appears from the scan that there are no additional internal injuries." He added that the heart, liver, and kidneys were functioning normally. Our most experienced orthopedic specialist, Dr. Peter Boman, was on duty when Lynn was admitted. He will update you regarding her condition once he's out of surgery."

Russ asked, "When do you think that will be?"

"Most likely in about a half hour."

Dr. Boman had seen many car accident victims. He needed to carefully weigh his words as he explained to the family the severity of his patient's injuries. He was tired. It had been a long day at the clinic ending back at the hospital. A forty-two-year old woman needed immediate surgery for multiple fractures sustained in a motor vehicle accident. Now he must face this woman's family and explain the gravity of her condition. Slowly he turned the corner and walked into the surgical waiting area, where many eyes looked up in anticipation.

He took a long breath, introduced himself, and then began. "The right side of Lynn's body sustained the most trauma. The right femur was broken, as well as, the right tibia, fibula, calcaneus, right humerus, and left ulna. I thought it best to wait to insert a titanium rod in the femur until Lynn stabilized. That could take a few days. Possible complications are blood clots forming by the fracture sites and traveling in the bloodstream to the brain, heart, or lung, causing a stroke. So, for now, we will place the right leg in traction and closely monitor her vital signs."

At first, Russ thought, Lynn's got a few broken bones, but she's going to be all right.

Then Dr. Boman spoke up. "I think you'd better stay the night at the hospital. Clearly, Lynn is in critical condition. If we get her through the night, we can be more optimistic."

Russell's heart dropped weighing down his chest like a ton of bricks, but he kept his composure. He told himself that he needed to be strong for the girls. They would keep an overnight vigil at the hospital. Lynn was tough. Plus, she had "sisu." She'll be okay.

Around midnight, the girls, along with Janet, got an opportunity to see Lynn before she was transferred from post-op to the intensive care unit. There wasn't a scratch on her face. Even her Berry Berry Nice lipstick remained perfectly applied. The van's airbag prevented major trauma to her head which her dad once said was only the size of an orange.

Prior to the accident, Lynn was a healthy, active forty-two-year-old woman. All of this factored into the doctor's decision to wait.

Time passed slowly for everyone. Periodically nurses came in to check on Lynn's condition. The family took turns funneling in and out of the ICU. Brooke and Amy flipped through dog-eared magazines, while Russ sat silently with his thoughts. Robyn curled up on the couch, trying to block out the world. Janet and mother-in-law, Jackie, whispered together on an adjacent sofa. It was a very long night.

CHAPTER 11

A Gracious Giver

It is well with the man who is gracious and lends,
who conducts his affairs with justice.
—Psalm 112:5 (NASB)

WHEN RAYMOND LOST HIS RIGHT eye from a rare disease, he was only twenty-one years old. Doctors predicted that his left eye would be spared if the diseased eye was removed. That proved to be true. Ray had only been married for two months.

Surgery was performed at a hospital in Minneapolis. Afterwards Ray and Millie returned to the Juntunen farmstead. Two months of recovery followed with Ray lying flat on his back for most of the day. His young wife, Mildred, became the around-the-clock nurse. She tenderly bathed and bandaged her beloved husband's eye. After several weeks, sutures were removed, and the incision healed. Ray was fitted with a glass eye. In later years, a plastic eye would replace the glass one.

Miraculously, for the next sixty-seven years, Ray learned to function quite well with only his left seeing eye. The prosthetic blended nicely into the youthful muscles surrounding his right socket. The only time the flesh drooped near that eye was when Ray was very tired.

Ed paid for the surgery performed in Minneapolis. Back then health insurance was nonexistent. Only cash, bartering, or monthly payment plans were accepted by the hospital and doctors.

Ray's eye doctor in Duluth, agreed to an unusual fee for his services. That said, instead of exchanging money, Millie and Ray tended goats and calves at Dr. Krohn's hobby farm, located up the North Shore near Finland, Minnesota. During that long, cold winter, the couple felt very isolated from their family but thankful they could work off the debt from the eye specialist.

Both Millie and Ray had never been away from their families for an extended period of time. As they spent the winter of 1941 in the quiet forest, both longed for the noise and confusion from their large brood. Midway through February, Mildred's sister and parents drove to the hobby farm for a visit. It was Mildred's twenty-first birthday. She cried when the cabin door opened; and there stood her mother, father, and sister Gladys. These welcomed guests eased the isolation and loneliness the couple was experiencing.

Before long, the March winds began to melt the snow from the glacial hillside. Crystal clear streams freely flowed down again toward Lake Superior. Dr. Knapp's goats and cows were restless after being penned up during the long Minnesota winter. Similarly, the young married couple was restless of being penned up as well. Once Easter Sunday arrived, they left the hobby farm debt-free with $200 in their pocket.

Debt was unheard of to Ray's father, Ed Juntunen. His credit was never questioned. With less than a fifth-grade education, Ed possessed acute math and accounting skills that helped him understand profit margins and milk production ratios. He had a business plan before the term was created. Ed paid cash for mostly everything; still there were times he bartered goods for services.

Often, people came to the farm needing money for an unexpected expense. Instead of going to the bank, the Finns helped out one another. Many banking institutions thought the immigrants were at risk since they had little or no collateral.

Ed Juntunen with his generous heart became known as a local lender. When a man had fallen on hard times or misfortune, he stopped by the farm looking for Ed. Giving good reasons for needing money, Ed rarely refused an impoverished soul. His Christian values never wavered when it came to giving.

Usually, he asked if they needed assurance that their sins were forgiven. This was the common verbiage used among Apostolic parishioners. Ed, with strong conviction, thought it important to address the issue of salvation with those who didn't share his beliefs.

These convictions were founded by Swedish Evangelist Lars Laestadian, who lived near Suomussalmi, Finland. He preached sin and salvation. It was black and white. Either you believed his way, or you were not assured a place in paradise. A dramatic conversion experience was necessary. Many of the Sami/Lapp population embraced Laestadian's teaching. During the mid 1800's his movement followed Finnish immigrants to the United States.

Laestadian was a charismatic, energetic man, who had an awakening after visiting a young girl named Maria of Lapland. She greatly challenged his faith and expressed that he should believe his sins forgiven and know God's peace. His spirit radically changed, and he was convicted to the belief where one must encounter a spiritual crisis leading to a conversion experience. He denounced dancing, instrumental music in worship, and alcoholic beverages, since alcoholism was epidemic among the Sami people. It was commonplace for men and women to come to his services intoxicated and unruly. This incensed the preacher and he sternly condemned any form of alcohol except wine when partaking of Holy Communion. Also, his doctrine forbade women from wearing jewelry or cutting their hair. His dogma filtered over to the States, and there was a great revival among Finnish settlers in the Upper Peninsula and Minnesota.

The Apostolic Lutheran Church was formed under Laestadian's philosophy. Services were very emotional with weeping and wailing, where ladies rolled in the church aisle, much like the Pentecostals of that era, who were called "holy rollers." This was a part of a religious ecstasy called "*liikutukset.*" A young impressionistic boy once claimed he witnessed a euphoric man climbing up the church pillar and barking like a dog…quite sure that young bystander embellished.

These new Finnish Americans were zealous in their pursuit to evangelize others.

Since Ed was a respected member of the Apostolic Church, he practiced evangelism when the opportunity arose. He truly was concerned for people's souls. The church doctrine suggested that the Apostolics alone possessed the "keys to the kingdom" and all who didn't believe their way were not "saved."

Yet, once "saved," the believer was constantly reminded of his sinfulness. Great importance was attached to adhering to the strict do's and don'ts of the law which, of course, were entirely impossible to keep. Hence, over and over again, congregants faced the consequences of not measuring up, feeling defeated and unworthy of God's blessings and favor. The conviction of God's judgment and damnation was discouraging, when works didn't measure up. The constant need to emotionally repent aloud to either a pastor or a layman was emphasized.

In actuality, most men didn't know how to respond to Ed's plea for absolution. The concept of repenting was the driving force when Ed asked if a person wanted the assurance that their sins were forgiven. Usually they responded to the invitation. This pleased Ed, who truly cared about the salvation of a lost soul.

So he would place his hand on their shoulder proclaiming, "Your sins are forgiven by the shed blood of Jesus."

Ed was grateful that the man had seen "the Light." But, that was not a stipulation for granting a loan. Instead, he perceived this as his Christian duty. Ed believed that he had an obligation to share "the Good News of salvation" in the same manner in which he, as a young man, had been converted.

Shortly thereafter, he'd go into his office, open the safe, and return with the money. Ed was happy when he could help out another man and his family. Ed never called up a debt from anyone. Even if the lendee failed to pay him back, he forgave the loan. This generosity would bring favor to Ed and his family. He lived by the scripture in Matthew: "Love God first and love your neighbor as yourself." He understood this concept and taught his family by example to do the same.

Today's Apostolic Churches have split into several factions, some with stricter guidelines for membership, sometimes shaming those who break from the group. The Esko Apostolic Church has moved past Laestadian's rigid rules and embraced the truth of God's word first, rebirth by the saving grace of Christ and the promise of eternal life for all who believe in Jesus. God's love is their motivating factor as a generous heart was the motivation for Ed Juntunen's lending ways so many years ago.

CHAPTER 12

Be Blessed and Bless Others

Blessed is the man who fears the Lord, who finds great
delight in His commandments. His children will be
mighty in the land; the generation of the upright will
be blessed. Wealth and riches are in His house.
—Psalm 112: 1-3 (NASB)

IN KEEPING WITH FINNISH TRADITION, aging Joseph now deferred
the homestead, that he and Elsa bought in 1885, to his eldest son
Ed and wife Esther. He lived out his life surrounded by family on
the land he so dearly loved. Ed, along with his father, Joseph, had
the foresight to first market potatoes. The rocky soil and cool northern Minnesota climate generated perfect growing conditions for root
vegetables. The boys missed weeks of school while they helped with
planting in the spring and picking in September. Teachers understood the fact that farmers needed their sons to help with crops. Most
of the potatoes were busheled into gunny sacks and transported to
town for market. The rest were hauled into the cool cellar and used
as a major staple at mealtime. Often, they were cooked for breakfast,
dinner, and supper.

Potatoes were a cash crop, and with the profits, Ed expanded
Meadowbrook Dairy. He bought more cows and sold more milk to
area stores. His sons worked alongside their father and looked to him
for direction and leadership. Saving a dollar or two was encouraged;

yet each of Ed's children understood the concept to freely give of your time, talent, and treasure whenever necessary.

During postwar America, the housing industry was booming; jobs were plentiful. Lynn's parents were able to live "the American Dream." Every month Ray and Mildred squirreled away a few extra dollars and earmarked the money for building their dream home. Yet, when the time came for the actual construction, they needed a loan. Ray sought his father's counsel.

Unfortunately, the timing was not favorable to borrow from Meadowbrook Dairy. Recently, the business acquired the nearby Lahti farm and was in the process of expanding the milk house and updating its equipment. These expenditures tapped cash reserves.

Pa suggested, "Why don't you ask Hjalmer for a loan. I'm sure he can help you out."

Ray had always felt a kindred spirit toward his uncle and didn't hesitate to visit the elder, who agreed to loan his nephew eight-hundred dollars. No documents were signed, only a verbal agreement and handshake made in good faith. Hjalmer trusted Ray and knew Mildred would make certain her husband delivered the monthly loan payment.

Like in the past, Finnish families continued to help one another and Mildred and Ray were very grateful for the opportunity to begin building a house across the road from Meadowbrook.

After looking through several house plans at Kinnunen Lumber, the couple made their decision and drew up a blueprint.

Next, they hired a Finnish carpenter to build the modest three-bedroom home. Ray, in his free hours away from the dairy, worked alongside craftsman Sulo Aho. In between household duties, Mildred helped the men shingle the roof, but later, developed a severe case of shingles. Through it all, the labor costs were cut in half because many family members lent a helping hand.

Financial security did not come without hard work and budgeting. Mildred continued to stash a few dollars from every monthly paycheck into the First National Bank in Cloquet where her father-in-law occupied a seat on its board of directors. Frugal Millie managed the finances and paid the monthly bills. Like his father, Ray had the final word involving major financial decisions. The one-income family was very common in the '50s. Some women worked outside the home as teachers or nurses, but the majority of Lynn's aunts stayed home as housewives.

Several of Ed's grandchildren, along with Lynn, thought the family, well, at least their grandfather, was rich. The Juntunens with Meadowbrook Dairy were the largest property owners in the small township claiming over four hundred acres of farmland.

As a youngster, Lynn walked in the fields singing the title song from the movie *The Exodus*.

"This land is mine. God gave this land to me—this brave and ancient land to me."

From the house and as far as her eye could see was Juntunen land. She believed the property indirectly belonged to her, and she was proud of her heritage that began with Joseph and her grandfather Andrew Edwin.

Grandpa Ed was a kind, generous man who trusted his instincts. Much like his father, Ed taught the little girl with crooked bangs the importance of living within your means, buying land, and saving money. Perhaps this mindset precipitated from the fact that Joseph and Elsa came to America practically penniless and wanted their heirs never to experience poverty. Perhaps they stressed the power of money almost as much as the power of God. The family would never know. But they did know this: above all, giving back to God and to others remained Ed's pedagogy. He lived by the Golden Rule: "Do unto others as you would have them do unto you."

From an early age, children learned that a penny saved is a penny earned and were encouraged to open savings accounts, deposit money, and collect interest.

Credit and debit cards with their high interest rates and fees were nonexistent at that time. Anyway, they would not have been acceptable by Ed's financial philosophy. But his acceptable spiritual philosophy never wavered.

And so it was. On a chilly Sunday evening in February of 1977, Ed dressed in all-wool worsted trousers, a shirt and tie and drove the mile and a half to the church. He looked forward to visiting his fellow parishioners before the informal service began. Once the minister, Ed's nephew Reverend Wayne Juntunen, took his place behind the podium, everyone quieted down and opened their hymnals to the familiar song "Amazing Grace."

Ed was seated in his pew, the fourth one on the right. Ever since anyone could remember, this member of their congregation occupied that same pew. As the hymn ended, Ed stood, turned around to face the parishioners and began to speak. He reviewed his life and faith, how as a young man he came under the conviction of sin and how difficult it is for a man to humble himself, acknowledge his sins, and ask for God's grace. He stressed the importance of keeping one's conscience clean.

Then he spoke from his heart, his voice trembling, "I want you to know how important it is that you believe in the Lord Jesus Christ and repent of your sins. And I, too, want to be assured that *my* sins are forgiven."

Ed was one of the most devout elders in the Apostolic Lutheran Church. Yet he needed this assurance.

From the pulpit, the pastor raised his arms toward his uncle Ed. Those nearest him laid their hands on the man's shoulders and spoke in unison, "Your sins are forgiven by his shed blood."

Then it was Ed's turn. He raised his arms and blessed everyone there, with a special exhortation for the children. After the blessing he slowly sat down in the pew and dropped his head to pray. He died right then and there in that church pew, the one he occupied ever since the church was built.

There was rejoicing in heaven that day and rejoicing in the church. Ed Juntunen was laid to rest three days later in the family burial plot next to Esther and his three sons, Thomas, Warren, and Leslie.

Still there was no rejoicing at Meadowbrook Dairy. The patriarch had died, and the brick house was quiet and empty. No longer could the "boys" meet with their father for morning coffee at the table in the kitchen. They had always looked for approval and guidance from him. His words were the assurance his sons needed.

Grief consumed Raymond especially when he walked into the barn...the place Ed visited every morning to discuss the daily plan. The father did not dictate every move at the farm. Instead Ray and he bounced ideas off one another.

"Do you think we should start baling hay today? Or should we sell the newest calf or add it to the herd?"

Those were ideas tossed around from father to son. And, oh, how Ray missed that interaction. Nevertheless, the "boys" needed to continue running the dairy business that the family had built up from Joseph's beginnings in 1885. And they did.

Although their father was no longer advising them, they had a commitment and responsibility to their children and grandchildren and their milk customers. For the next ten years, Meadowbrook Dairy, Inc. ran efficiently and was profitable. Ed's sons continued delivering milk to area residences, grocery and convenience stores. They bought nearby land when longtime owners were ready to sell. The Maaranen's i.e. Carlsons's and Edgar Olson's farmsteads added an additional one-hundred acres to Meadowbrook. As in the days of Joseph, land acquisition remained at the forefront. Still, the rigors of dairy farming were continually evolving with stricter federal regulations, and more advanced technology. Taking these factors into consideration, the brothers wondered how much longer they wanted to continue working.

In the meantime, Ray suffered a Transient Ischemic Attack, a mini stroke, while he was walking to the barn for early milking. Even though he lost his vision in one eye, Ray navigated to the apple tree by the milk house. Slowly sight returned as he made his familiar way along the circular driveway. Only after chores were done did he return home to tell Mildred what happened. Without hesitation she rushed him to the Emergency Room in Cloquet. Because of the temporary blindness, Ray was abruptly transferred by ambulance to a Duluth hospital. He was admitted and tests confirmed the TIA diagnosis. The neurologist at St. Luke's Hospital prescribed a blood thinner and after three days Ray was discharged.

Being the quintessential minimalist, Ray told everyone, "I just had the flu, that's all."

Besides Ray's TIA, several other clues pointed to the fact that Ed's sons were aging and nearing retirement. The effects of heavy farm labor, the long hours coupled with their advancing ages prompted them to sell the dairy business. The corporation dissolved, yet Meadowbrook Dairy remained in the family. In 1981 nephew Dale traded his accountant pens for calf pens. The purchase included Meadowbrook Dairy, the livestock, equipment, creamery, including most of the land. The five uncles agreed to the sale with one stipulation. They could work there for as long as they wished. However, six years later all but one had formally retired. Dale and his wife Joanne continued to farm and sell milk to the public until 1989.

The barn, now empty, was a reminder of the past, and the tattered milk house remained a testament to the many hours Lynn's father and uncles supplied the local area with one of the most essential commodities…milk.

The little girl was thankful for the lessons she learned witnessing a successful family enterprise where Joseph, Ed, and sons worked cohesively. She watched how unselfishly they assumed specific roles in the family business. But "time and tide wait for no man" and before long the men grew old and Meadowbrook Dairy was no more. Yet, in their time, they chose happiness and appreciation for a livelihood that began over one-hundred years earlier, when Joseph and Elsa settled in the quaint Finnish community Lynn Rae called "home."

CHAPTER 13

Waiting in the Waiting Room

Wait for the Lord; be strong and let your heart
take courage; yes, wait for the Lord.
—Psalm 27:14 (NASB)

THE SEVENTH FLOOR BECAME THE *family's meeting place. The hours
slipped by into days. The phone kept ringing in the waiting room as family
and friends inquired about the condition of the patient. Pastors from
both Lutheran churches in Esko, Reverend Ray Hilman and Reverend
Norman Aman, returned nearly every day to offer support and prayers.*

*Many visitors were received by the family. A student of Russ's made a
surprise appearance after school one day. Usually disheveled and looking
for a laugh in class, he strolled into the hospital wearing a white shirt and
tie with his hair neatly combed. He clutched in his hand a bouquet of
stargazer lilies from the Applied Math class that Russ taught during seventh hour. This young man, who, on several occasions, had been scolded
in the classroom, now showed his tender heart while hugging his teacher.*

*Hours passed. Days became nights, and the lives of Lynn's family
centered around hospital events.*

*Brother-in-law Danny went on a fact-finding mission to the
Douglas County Sheriff's Office. He was given a copy of the accident
report and was told where to find the demolished van. He took several
pictures of the vehicle and gathered the rest of Lynn's belongings from
the wreckage. Dan wondered how his sister-in-law made it out of that*

crushed van and was still alive. He continued driving along Highway 35 to the accident site. The pavement was marked with skid lines from tires. Glass littered the shoulder of the highway. Most certainly there had been a horrific accident on that road. There were no casualties...yet.

Back at the hospital, Lynn remained in critical condition, while the other driver, Grace, and her children were released. This mother and her two children had been going to the Superior courthouse for a custody hearing on February 8. They never got there.

Local newspapers and television stations picked up the story and broadcast it throughout the tristate area. The police report was public information and was considered newsworthy.

The Esko school, area churches, and community supported Lynn's family during this very difficult time. People came to the hospital to show their concern and love. For a time, Russ asked the nurses to restrict visitors when it became overwhelming to usher each person into the ICU to see Lynn.

Day after day florists made deliveries to the woman in critical condition. Unfortunately, the beautiful plants and floral displays were prohibited from entering her ICU cubicle. Instead, the blossoms were displayed on a table outside the doorway where the sweet floral scents wafted throughout the sterile hallway.

Hundreds of get well cards arrived at the hospital. The words of encouragement cheered Lynn. Since both arms were broken, she needed someone to hold and read the cards to her. This patient was very limited in what she could do. She had to be fed, bathed, and cared for like a total invalid. This once independent woman needed help with just about everything. How that humbled her.

CHAPTER 14

The Sunnarborg Homestead

Grandchildren are a crown of old men; and
parents are the pride of their children.
—Proverbs 17:6 (NASB)

SOME THOMSON TOWNSHIP RESIDENTS BELIEVED that the closer your property was to Esko's Corner, the more valuable. The Sunnarborg farm was located about two miles north of the corner. Many Finnish families owned land in the northern region of the township and that was where Johan Eric Sunnarborg settled. When relatives immigrated in 1882 from Finland around the time of the Civil War, the last name was changed from Sunnari to Sunnarborg. Johnan Eric married Anna Sofia Kuuvela, and together they had seven children, five sons and two daughters. As a young man, he avoided military service during World War l because he was blind in one eye. John Eric, who was commonly known as Erick Sunnarborg, became a widower at age fifty-eight.

Shortly, after his wife, Anna Sofia, passed away in 1920, Erick left Thomson Township and his farm, and moved to Berkley, California. Once there, he remarried a widow, Matilda Nissinen Juukila. Rumor has it that he was waltzing Matilda years earlier when she lived in Superior, Wisconsin. Yet that was only a rumor.

The two remained on the West Coast living the high life party-ing with Hollywood actors. The new Mrs. Erick Sunnarborg's niece was actress Marian Nixon, who married renowned director William Seiter.

Often, the Sunnarborgs were listed in the Berkley Daily Gazette social columns entertaining actors and producers. William Seiter's first major hit was *Sons of the Desert* considered by many to be Laurel and Hardy's best feature films. He also directed Fred Astaire, Ginger Rogers, Shirley Temple, Barbara Stanwyck, as well as the Marx Brothers.

To maintain the Hollywood lifestyle, Erick needed money. Therefore, he decided to "sell" his farm in Thomson Township to eldest son John Erick II. He never acknowledged and honored the tradition where the eldest son inherits the farm. Instead, he wanted payment for the property. Erick was not in a position to finance his son and expected John to find money elsewhere.

The California newlyweds arrived in Duluth by train to finalize the sale of the homestead. John stood waiting for them in the Depot and was shocked to see that his stepmother was very attractive. He expected her to be matronly, gray haired, and old. Instead, Matilda's skin was smooth without wrinkles, and she was luxuriously dressed in a fur coat and matching hat. She noticed that John's clothes were tattered and worn. After exchanging pleasantries, the three rode in silence back to the farm. John wondered if his father expected a higher price for the farm than he could afford.

When the trio arrived in the old Model A, they were met by five smiling youngsters squealing with delight to once again see their grandfather. He fumbled in his pants pocket and placed a white peppermint into each child's soiled little hand. Erick was slightly embarrassed with their exuberance yet secretly happy they were excited to see him. Unbeknown to him, candy was their motivation for joy, not Pappa Eerikki.

Fannie, expecting her sixth child, opened the front door to welcome them. Then quickly wiped her wet hands on an apron before she shook the soft manicured hand of her mother-in-law. Fannie glanced up at John, who knew exactly what she was thinking.

This new mother-in-law was slim and beautiful, while sweet Fannie appeared uncomfortably round and pregnant. "How do you do?" the lady quipped. "I need to freshen up. Where's your lavatory?"

"Aaah, the outhouse is back there," Erick answered while nervously pointing his finger to the backyard. "I'll show you."

His wife spun around in a huff and marched off to the privy following Erick. The children snickered as Fannie shooed them off to continue their game of hide-and-seek.

When the new Mrs. Sunnarborg returned, she hissed to her husband, "There was no toilet paper in that foul, rancid outhouse, so I used my lace handkerchief to wipe my bottom and threw it down that hole! Now you're going to buy me a new one when we return to California."

In short, the visit began with an offensive smell and grew stinkier as the day progressed.

Early the next morning, John drove the Model A to the Cloquet Co-op Credit Union and was told that he qualified for a hundred-year farmer's loan. The small payments would be manageable, and the mortgage could be paid back earlier without penalty. He secured the cash and delivered the first payment in a manila envelope to his father. Erick and his bride left the next morning. His grandchildren were ecstatic. They had been on pins and needles, afraid their behavior would be unacceptable to their PaPa and his new wife, Matilda. Fannie felt sad at her father-in-law's departure. By living so far away in California, he never would get to know her delightful children.

Two years later, Erick and his city slicker wife reluctantly returned to Thomson Township to get another farm payment. Sweet Fannie tried to be a welcoming hostess to her in-laws. It was very clear the woman disliked her husband's family and their living conditions. The visits were very short.

Contrary to Matilda's opinion, the Sunnarborgs were a self-respecting and ambitious family and never accepted the notion that they were in need of anything. John worked a variety of jobs as the township road boss, part-time logger, well driller, farmer, and jack of all trades. Also, he exercised his civic duties by serving on the Thomson (Esko) School Board during construction of the Lincoln

High School. His name, along with the other board members, was engraved on the building's cornerstone.

John never fully repaid the one-hundred-year farm loan he secured from the credit union. He died. Years later, his bachelor son Martin, who lived all of his life on the farm, paid off his father's debt. Yet shortly after the bank loan was satisfied, Martin died from a massive heart attack while shoveling snow by the mailbox.

During the '40s and '50s John farmed the land with the help of his sons. He bought two draft horses, Queen and Mae. They were perfectly paired, and John expertly handled the Percherons. For additional income, he hauled lumber from the northern camps and maintained township equipment and roads, being promoted to "Road Boss." He plowed snow in the winter and graded roads in the summer.

John was industrious and mechanically inclined. That gift was inherited by his six sons. He could fix any broken piece of machinery and wasn't afraid to try. He spoke a colorful language which his sons quickly learned to mimic. John was a proud man and even prouder of his large family.

Both Fannie and John lived out their gift of hospitality. The little girl remembered that whenever someone stopped by the farmhouse, the cordial woman made sure that they were fed. Without hesitation she rushed into the well-stocked pantry, then opened the small Frigidaire icebox. With short quick motions she grabbed what she needed, then proceeded to whip up a fine lunch for the visitors. Likewise, if a man stopped by and needed a place to sleep for the night, John invited him to stay. Regrettably, lice came along with the boarder. When they departed, the lice remained and made their way to the children's hair. But Ma came to the rescue. She marched onto the back porch, got out the can of kerosene, and poured it over the heads of the children. Oh, how it stung the scalp as fumes burned in their nostrils!

Although the Sunnarborg family was not rich, they never went hungry. Like most of the local men, John made a weekly trip to Esko's Corner for groceries and the much needed supplies. He traded eggs and milk for flour, sugar, children's shoes, wool yarn, and fabric.

Sometimes oldest daughter Mildred accompanied her father to town to Juntti's Store. After they finished bartering and buying supplies, the two stood by the candy counter. Looking through the glass at the confectionery, Mildred's eyes sparkled with excitement. John proudly beamed as he looked over at his daughter and asked Mr. Juntti, "Put a few peppermints in the bag for the girl, Eino. *Kiitos paljon*"

If the red meat supply was scarce, venison was always plentiful.

John directed one of the boys, "Ma needs deer meat for supper. Go shoot one in the back forty."

They didn't have to be asked twice to hunt and, before long, they returned with fresh venison for the family.

Most of the time, Fannie remained at home. Yet, on occasion, she interrupted housework to visit a neighbor or attend a church service. The woman never complained. She cooked, canned, and sewed the children's clothes by using newspapers as tracing paper for the patterns. Holding the paper up against the child's back, the clever seamstress estimated the approximate size, then cut and stitched away until a perfect pair of pajamas or trousers was ready for wear.

Her work was never done. Whenever possible, the three oldest daughters, Mildred, Gladys, and Alice helped their mother. These daughters not only did the household chores; they also went into the barn and tended to the milking, as was the old Finnish custom. While tending the cows, the girls tended to singing songs.

Beautiful Fannie Carlson was born in Thomson Township in 1890. She was the daughter of Frederick and Mary (Holm) Carlson. Her grandparents were Karl and Anna Grethe Eriksson. Some of Karl's children moved to Norway and Sweden while others booked passage to the United States.

After being hired to work on Norwegian fishing boats, "*loskar og fisker*," Fannie's father Frederick decided to immigrate to the USA in 1882. He was twenty-six years old. Three years after arriving in Thomson Township, he married Mary Holm, who was six years older. Fannie's parents changed their name to Carlson in an attempt to Americanize while two of Frederick's sons used the name Maaranen which was a geographical location in the general area of their birthplace.

In fact, most of Fannie's family members were very honored to be American citizens. The mother always spoke English to her children. She reasoned to them that they were born and lived in the Unites States, not Finland. Their lineage dated back to the Sami or Lap tribe. The Sami claimed to be the aboriginal Northern Europeans, possibly those who first reentered Europe from the Ice Age. The genetic origin of the Sami was unknown but many historians agree that the Sami represented an Asian and European population. Their darker skin tones and almond eyes differed from the majority of blonde fair-skinned Scandinavians.

The majority of Sami people settled along the inland river, along the fjords and on the outer coast. Fishing in the seawater or in freshwater, and hunting and herding of cows, sheep, and reindeer made up the livelihood of most Sami.

Fannie's grandfather Karl Eriksson grew up ten miles east of Karesuando in the small town of Kuttainen on the Muonio River. The family earned their livelihood through reindeer husbandry, fishing, and farming. These skills were carried over to America along with the religious movement embraced in northern Lapland

Karesuando was a well-known church town where in the 1840s Lars Levi Laestadius served as pastor. He greatly altered the religious practices of the Sami people. He preached with much animosity toward the authorities and the State church.

The Carlsons and Sunnarborgs did not adapt to the strict and puritan teachings from this religious awakening. Instead, Fannie read daily from the Finnish family bible and had a deep intercessory prayer ministry. She retreated to her bedroom and once there, expressed her devotion to Jesus, as well as, her petitions for her family's well-being.

All twelve children were baptized and confirmed in the Apostolic Lutheran Church and lived out their faith with big-hearted actions instead of mere words. The men were gruff, but that was a façade to cover their very sensitive nature. The women were resilient and generous like their mother Fannie, who exemplified the pioneer spirit.

CHAPTER 15

Back to ICU

Be anxious for nothing but in everything by prayer and supplication
with thanksgiving, let your requests by made known to God.
—Philippians 4:6 (NASB)

EVERY DAY, FRIENDS AND FAMILY *continued to come to the hospital bearing gifts of food, candy, and flowers. Mostly though, they brought their love and concern for not only Lynn but also for her husband and daughters. In the meantime, for spiritual nourishment, hospital clergy and lay ministers offered Holy Communion to the patient.*

Usually, Janet, Russ, or one of her daughters fed soft foods to Lynn, whose arms were immobile. Once upon a time, she spooned baby food into her daughters' little mouths. Now they were giving her pureed peaches or noodles to slowly swallow.

Morphine was making Lynn speak rudely to the hospital staff. Once a woman from housekeeping was dusting the window ledges, and Lynn demanded, "Can't you move a little faster?"

Another time a nurse's aide was checking Lynn's catheter, and Lynn blurted out to Russ, "She's dumb as a rock!"

The patient needed drugs for pain control, yet after they were administered to Lynn, she had no filter. Russ kept apologizing to the hospital staff for his wife's behavior. They were doing their job quite well. As a patient, Lynn's patience was being tested.

One week passed, and on Monday, the doctor ordered Lynn to be transferred out of ICU. A registered nurse in charge of the unit completed paperwork while certified nursing assistants unhooked cords and packed up her belongings. Two orderlies wheeled Lynn on a gurney to a private room on the fourth floor. Rolling through the hospital hallways, she stared at the ceiling tiles as they blurred past her eyes. The gurney wheels came to a halt and then turned into a bright sunlit room.

It was Valentine's Day. Russ's sweetheart was "out of the woods," and the family celebrated with a delicious casserole sent over by Lynn's godmother, Inga.

Later that evening, the Esko varsity girls played a basketball game at Moose Lake. The Eskomos won by three points 49-46. Brooke was the senior captain of the team. Russ, his parents, Lynn's parents, Janet, and Danny all went to the game to cheer on Brooke, while Robyn stayed at the hospital with her mom. The two watched the Winter Olympics where the drama with Nancy Kerrigan and Tonya Harding was unfolding. While at the ball game, many concerned spectators sought out Russ to ask about Lynn and her current condition. Over and over, he repeated much of the same information. He didn't mind and understood that they had been praying not only for Lynn but also for him and his daughters.

That night, for the first time in a very long time, Russ slept. He awoke the next morning refreshed, and knowing that Lynn was no longer in ICU, he decided to get back to his students and teaching math. The teacher had a renewed spring in his step as he walked to school. This Tuesday began in a comfortable manner which had been very absent for the past six days since the accident.

Robyn was still in Esko but planned to return the next day to her retail management job in Minneapolis. About nine o'clock in the morning, the telephone woke her. A nurse from St. Mary's Hospital asked for Russ Davidson. Robyn told her that he was at work. She asked Robyn's relationship to Lynn. Then, reluctantly, the nurse explained that doctors believed Lynn had a stroke. Additional tests were being administered to determine the source.

Just as soon as she hung up from the hospital, Robyn called the school and asked, "Can you please get Russ Davidson from his classroom? It is urgent."

From over the PA system, the secretary summoned Russ to the main office for the phone call. No telephones were in classrooms. He ran down the long hallway fearing the worst.

Robyn told him he needed to get to the hospital and fast. It was very possible that Mom had a stroke.

"Whaaat?" Russ shouted into the phone. "Mom was doing so well!"

Quickly, Russ tracked down Brooke and Amy and pulled them out of their first-hour classes. The high school principal, Mr. Berglund, offered to drive them to the hospital. Russ and the girls were reeling in shock as they stepped into his car. Once again, their emotions were unraveling for fear of the unknown. The high school principal knew that his passengers needed consoling. As his hands held the steering wheel, his heart held a prayer. Solemnly, he asked God's wisdom and guidance for the doctors and comfort for this family. Then to himself, he wondered how much more could they endure.

CHAPTER 16

Kissin' Cousins

"As for you, be fruitful and multiply and fill the earth."
—Genesis 9:7 (NASB)

THOUSANDS OF MOMENTS SLIPPED INTO days, weeks, and years. During the next two decades, another generation arrived.

There were twelve children begotten of John and Fannie Sunnarborg. All married except Martin. The grand total, including spouses, equaled twenty aunts and uncles on Lynn's mother's side.

Ray's parents, Ed and Esther, bore sixteen children with two dying in infancy. Tommy never married, and Verna opted not to have children. Still, twelve of Ed and Esther's children chose matrimony and parenthood.

Lynn's forty-two aunts and uncles were rapidly filling the family tree with fresh, young leaves, which totaled seventy-one first cousins.

Lynn bonded particularly well to the ones closest to her age. The children spent many hours entertaining one another. They played together, fought together, made up, and then resumed play. The bond of blood was thick; family mattered. A profound loyalty toward one another defined their relationships.

Later on, this unwavering loyalty became a catalyst which propelled Lynn and many of her cousins toward successful professional, as well as individual accomplishments. The personal mission statement of strong Finnish work ethic and confidence was deeply ingrained into these young lives. They had "*sisu*."

Yet, for the time being, the cousins were merely rambunctious children frolicking like calves in the pasture. They lived the carefree, innocent life while creating innovative ways to play. Work would be required later on as it had for their parents.

When the Juntunen men finished chores at the dairy, they slowly walked back to their homes…another day over, another dollar earned by these hardworking dads. Families sat around the table and dined together enjoying a hearty meal. This was the norm for them.

Once the dishes were washed, dried, and put back into the cupboards, the cousins left the kitchen and ran posthaste out the door to play. The classic game of hide-and-seek was quite challenging around the many outbuildings on the farm. Whoever was "it" had a difficult time finding the others, because there were so many great places to hide. From behind doors and narrow spots, a small child could easily disappear. However, there was an unspoken rule. The milk house with its walk-in cooler was off-limits.

Climbing up the narrow wooden ladder to the hayloft was scary yet exhilarating. The cousins peered down from the highest windows in the barn. It seemed as if they could see the whole world from those heights. Sunlight streamed through the narrow cracks to reveal hay dust filtering into the air. The sweet smell of alfalfa and clover tickled their noses.

If there weren't enough cousins available to play games, Warren and Lynn resorted to finding other projects. On one occasion, the two pretended to be chemists, concocting a thick gray substance that they christened "Man Killer." They combined ingredients from barrels of disinfectants, fertilizers, and oil found in the farm garage. The two, with wide-eyed innocence, watched the bubbling chemical reaction. It was a miracle that an explosion didn't occur from mixing together all those toxic components. Surely, the two mad scientists had a guardian angel. Man Killer might possibly have killed them.

Farther past the garage the Midway River seemed to beckon youngsters during every season. During the winter months of the 1930s, young Ray and his brothers could hardly wait until the ice was thick enough for skating. The shallow water down from the rapids froze quickly and became the perfect site for the rink. The children strapped on the makeshift skates and cleared any snow from the ice. The boys formed hockey sticks from thick willow branches while using an old sole of a leather shoe for the puck. Neighbor boy Edgar Olson was the fastest skater, and everyone wanted him on their team. On the other hand, his younger cousin Millard was rather slow; he was usually designated as the goalie.

Much like their fathers, the next generation of Juntunen children established a skating rink in the same shallow spot along the river. First ice sometimes occurred as early as Thanksgiving. The cousins cleared snow from the surface with shovels and banked the sides, forming a large rectangle. Then they glided along the frozen water, playing games similar to the ones their dads played thirty years before. Up and down and around they'd go across the glassy sheet of ice. The crisp air filled their rosy cheeks and lungs. After several hours, the little girl and her cousins plopped on a snowbank exhausted yet at the same time exhilarated. The worst part was yanking the skates off tired, numb feet, then trudging back home. The best part was the hot cocoa with marshmallows that was waiting for them on the stove in the warm kitchen.

During hot summer days, the swimming hole two hundred yards west of Grandpa Ed's brick house became the hangout for everyone. The rippling waters were a source of cool refreshment, as well as a gathering hub to socialize. Mothers from all over the township parked their cars along the Juntunen Road. Children tumbled out from the backseats anxious to cool off in the Midway's water that looked like a triillion gallons of ice tea. From Memorial Day until the dog days of summer, the river was *the* place to be on a hot summer afternoon. Walking down to the river's edge and through the pasture, everyone was careful to dodge the myriad of cow pies along the way. Older kids jumped off the wooden bridge right into the deep. It was considered a triumph once a child was able to swim solo to the Big Rock, which marked the middle of the swimming hole.

Underwater tag was a favorite swimming game. The Meadowbrook cousins were all strong swimmers. When other kids

90

from the community came to their swimming hole, they were designated to be "it" first. Competition was fierce. Lynn prided herself in keeping up with the boys, holding her breath and swimming just as fast as anyone. Already gender equality was in its infant stages among this generation. Lynn wondered why some of the boys didn't like her. Obviously, they did not like to lose to a girl.

The "little kids," before they knew how to swim, played in the shallow water by the island. They chased minnows and picked shells and rocks from the bottom of the river. The moms sat closely by and suntanned, gossiped, and occasionally yelled out to a child who misbehaved.

When a mother was ready to pack up and leave, she shouted, "In five minutes, you'll have to get out of the water."

After five minutes, she'd yell again, "Okay, kids, get out now!"

Her children remained in the river.

Consecutive ultimatums were given every two to three minutes, but to no avail.

Finally, the frustrated mother marched into the water, grabbed her child by the arm, and threatened, "We're never coming back to the river ever again if you won't listen to me!"

This was a clear sign that they were in big trouble. Yet every child understood that on summer afternoons when the sun grew hot and the air muggy, mothers acquiesced by returning to the cool, refreshing waters of the Midway.

The family dog Sparky, a border collie, tried to be the lifeguard on the river. He was determined to protect the children and wouldn't allow swimmers near the fast moving current that he considered dangerous. He sprang into the river and swam around and around in the deep while barking furiously. Finally, two people would have to pull the smelly wet dog from the water and coax him up to the garage, where the "lifeguard" was held hostage until suppertime, when swimming dispersed for an hour.

Before long, there was no need for Sparky to protect the swimming hole, since it closed to the residents of the township. A horrible tragedy left a nine-year-old neighbor boy dead after he was crushed by a huge boulder.

Often, rock piles were located in the middle of any field. It was no different on the Juntunen properties where years earlier boulders were pulled out from the earth with the help of the mammoth, horses, chains, and a crowbar. The Juntunen men joked that there were more rocks in those fields than stars in the sky.

Yet, one autumn afternoon, moving rocks should've been left to men not to young lads. Very innocently, buddies Larry and Barry decided to dig a tunnel through the rock pile near the southwest forty. The boys grunted and pushed at the huge stones, rolling some to the left, some to the right. They were making great progress, so they thought, when Larry stretched his arms to dig out a smaller stone from the tunnel. Without warning, the tunnel collapsed, and a large boulder rolled over the boy's body. He screamed for his friend to help him. Barry tried with all of his might to roll away the stone that was crushing Larry. When he realized his efforts were futile, Barry dashed through the oat field and the shallow river by the cow crossing, then trudged up, up, up the steep hill to the farm yard.

The guys were milking the cows as the boy raced into the barn breathless from running and stammered, "A rock rolled on, Larry!"

"Where?" asked Ray.

"On the rock pile across the river," Barry cried tearfully.

Ray jumped up from behind the cow stall and hollered to Barry, "Get Grandpa to call the operator and report there's been an accident!"

Then Ray, along with Dick, the hired hand, left the milking parlor and raced to the blue '62 Chevy pickup. Ray quickly slid behind the steering wheel and drove as fast as he dared across the river to the southwest forty. As the two men approached the rock pile, Ray felt a sick feeling in his gut.

They found the nine-year-old boy no longer breathing, his young body still warm.

Four days later, Larry was buried this time in a pale blue casket at the St. Matthew's Church cemetery on the North Road.

Mrs. Lyes, his fourth-grade teacher, never mentioned Larry's name again to her students. Lynn wondered why no one talked about his death. They all knew he died in the rock pile on Meadowbrook.

The desk where he once sat remained empty for the rest of the school year. Once in a while, the little girl with crooked bangs glanced over to the vacant spot where Larry learned his multiplication facts, but never had to use them.

The Puotinen Family settled their lawsuit against Meadowbrook Dairy out of court. Gene Puline dug massive holes with his backhoe and buried all the rock piles that stood for almost a hundred years on the land that Joseph and Elsa retained back in 1885.

The Juntunen family, devastated by this tragedy, had no other option but to close the Midway River swimming hole to the public. "No Trespassing" signs were posted, and only family members were allowed access to the water from a gated entrance.

CHAPTER 17

Blood is Thicker Than Water

Cast your bread upon the waters, for you
will find it after many days.
—Ecclesiastes 11:1 (NASB)

THE SUNNARBORG FARM CONSISTED OF eighty acres of pasture and woodlands. A large red barn housed a dozen cows, loose hay in the loft, guinea hens, goats, and whatever Pa or the boys would bring back to the farm. A gray stone milk house kept the new milk cool and fresh. Wood was chopped every day and carried from the woodshed into the box in the kitchen. The Queen Bengal woodstove had a cast-iron surface with a top warming oven. Fannie regulated it with expert proficiency.

The farmhouse was remodeled in 1935 with a long narrow porch along the exterior south wall. Mildred and Martin painted the wood siding a milky white and planted clover seed next to the porch. The entrance door lead into the heart of the home, the kitchen. Almost everyone gathered around the table covered with a colorful oilcloth. A sturdy rocking chair was reserved for Fannie or her husband, John, who sometimes could be seen rocking one of the younger children and later his grandchildren.

Inside the lower left cupboard was a brown bag of *korpus*, a Finnish cinnamon toast. Next to the bag was a small white stoneware bowl of softened butter. Any child could help themselves to a *korpu* and slather it with a thick layer of soft yellow butter. To quench their thirst, the child pushed a wooden stool up to the white porcelain farmhouse sink and reached for the communal drinking cup. By turning the spigot of the small faucet, ice-cold water splashed into the cup.

"It's the best-tasting water in the township," boasted Pa.

The deep well was hand dug by John with the help of son Lloyd. In the latter years, John invested in a well driller and the father-son duo drilled many wells for area homeowners. The business of Sunnarborg Well Drilling was birthed and eventually expanded to include four generations of Sunnarborg men with Lloyd's son Craig successfully at the helm. Yet none surpassed the quality of the water that flowed from the faucet of the Sunnarborg kitchen sink.

Strong, hot ARCO coffee simmered in the heavy white pot resting quietly on the wood-burning stove. A cup was offered to every guest who walked into Fannie's kitchen. When the men came in, she hastily shuffled her short thin legs to the old icebox for *mukkada*, a bologna. Then she grabbed a sharp butcher knife from the second drawer and sliced freshly baked rye bread, *limppu*, to serve each guest. Her hospitality was renowned in the community. Nobody left hungry from Fannie's kitchen.

The basement was hand dug with walls of field stone and mortar. Wooden steps led to the sauna that was dark and damp. Every Saturday night, the sauna stove was heated with dry birch logs. As was the custom, the women and children bathed first. Worn scatter rugs covered the dressing room bench and narrow wood slats rested along the cement floor. A dimly lit bulb shown through the sooty window into the sauna. Large galvanized pails held water that was thrown onto the hot stones. As steam billowed high into the air, folks sat in stillness on top the wooden benches and breathed in the hot vapors. Inhibitions were released along with the steam and sweat.

Fannie's homemade pine soap made from lye and animal tallow was used to wash everyone from soft baby's skin to the boys' greasy stained hands. The men "took sauna" last when the stove was the hottest. By the close of the day, everyone was clean, refreshed, and ready for a good night's sleep.

Some Sundays, John hitched the horses to the wagon and drove Fannie and the girls to church. He thought religion was overrated and rarely attended services...not that he was an atheist. No, he worshipped God in his own way.

"I don't need to sit for hours in a pew and get all emotional," he quipped.

Truth be told, he had such a tender heart that he hid his sensitivity by being loud and gruff.

Along the way, John had been hurt. His father was a very insensitive man. Soon after his wife died, Erick left Thomson Township for the West Coast. He spent money frivolously and quickly remarried a woman. Shortly thereafter, John was blindsided by his father, who demanded quick payment for a farm that should've been handed down to his firstborn son, John. Old World Finns bequeathed their homestead to the firstborn son and then lived with his family until death. Because Erick relocated to California, he had no intention of permanently returning to Thomson Township. Sadly, John didn't inherit the land. Instead, he was given the first option to buy the homestead. Although John and Fannie were frugal people, they did not have a large nest egg saved. Their twelve children needed shoes and coats and food to eat. Reluctantly, John went to the bank and secured a loan for the Sunnarborg farm.

A large white barn housed a dozen Guernsey cows, a bull, and ten calves, including a chicken coop in the back. The girls were in charge of collecting eggs every day while Martin milked the cows.

On the fifteenth day of September 1941, lightning struck the barn roof, and a fire broke out. John and his sons attempted to get the horses and cows from their stalls and extinguish the flames. Regrettably, the fire could not be contained, and the family watched as the structure burned to the ground. Yet while the blaze crackled and spit glowing embers into the night sky, daughter Gladys, inside the farmhouse, was in labor, while her husband Leo helped his father-in-law fight fire. Amidst the sadness of a barn burning down, there was joy that night. For with the help of the local midwife, Gladys gave birth to a healthy baby boy, whom they named Russell. Her little sister Lola remembered the night very well. She heard cries of agonizing labor contractions from her sister and cries of sadness and loss from her mother. Still, the family counted their blessings and faced the fiery trial head-on.

Several days later, a crew of local men arrived at the farm for an old-fashioned barn raising. Later in the day the wives arrived bringing plenty of food and drink for the workers. With tools in hand and a spirit of giving, they rebuilt the barn from the ashes to the highest peak.

Although there was a time to work, there also was a time to play. The Sunnarborgs knew all about games and competition. John and Fannie's children passed down their love of sports to their children. They played softball, football, and basketball in warmer weather. Then during the winter months, just as soon as ice froze on the nearby pond, the kids skated and played Pom-Pom Pull-Away. The cousins were naturally athletic and strong. The little girl with crooked bangs was challenged by their raw talent and passion to win.

She loved this rugged, unsophisticated clan who called a spade a spade. They were quick-witted, intelligent, yet quick to anger. Remarkably, she was drawn to their unwavering loyalty to one another. And above all else, they knew how to have fun.

CHAPTER 18

The Day to Day Routine

She looks well to the ways of her household
and does not eat the bread of idleness.
—Proverbs 31:27 (NASB)

THERE WAS A ROUTINE IN the '50s and '60s that housewives followed well, at least most in the small township where Lynn grew up.

Lynn's mother conducted the day-to-day operations of the household. She purchased all the groceries, paid the bills, shopped for the families' clothes, and then laundered them. In her spare time, she sewed dresses, lingerie, and knitwear. On evenings, while sitting in a chair watching TV, she crocheted Afghans or knit wool mittens, slippers, and sweaters.

Mildred worked quickly and efficiently while juggling several tasks at one time. She made any excuse to be outdoors, and her gardening skills were renowned throughout the township. She exhibited her flowers, knitwear, and canned goods at the Esko Fair which was held annually on the second Thursday and Friday of August. By the end of that month, neatly packed jars of canned peaches, pears, dill pickles, and vegetables lined the pantry shelves, waiting to be opened in the dead of winter. Apples were gathered from Carlson's orchard, and on a good year, raspberries were abundant near the fence lines and rock piles. The marshes behind Moilanens' farmland were filled with blueberry bushes. Before bears arrived to pillage, the juicy deep-azure berries were picked, cleaned, and canned for sauces and pies.

Certain days of the week were delegated for certain chores.

The laundry was done on Monday. Before Ray returned from morning milking, the conventional washing machine in the basement was thumping away. The clothes, towels, and bedding were separated according to colors and pushed down into the washtub of water with a smooth wooden pole about three feet long. Stubborn stains were treated with Fels-Naptha soap, or Hi-Lex liquid bleach. Cheer powdered laundry detergent was sprinkled upon the waters as the ritual continued. When the washing cycle ended, the clothes were rinsed and pulled through a wringer, squeezing out excess water. If you bent over too close to the conventional machine, a mishap might occur. That is how the phrase "Don't get your tit in a wringer" was coined.

Mildred's mother, Fannie, almost lost her life while washing clothes. One morning, she was determined to begin the mountain of laundry and made her way onto the side porch where a gas-powered washer sat. Except on that particular Monday, it was in a cantankerous mood. The little woman started up the motor and began loading the top with bedding. Blue-gray smoke puffed from the motor as it sputtered along. Fannie felt nauseous and crumpled down onto the hard cement floor. The motor continued to fill the tiny room with carbon monoxide. As husband John walked from the milkhouse to the nearby garage, he heard the washer making unfamiliar sounds and decided to check it out. He approached the side porch only to see his wife passed out on the cold floor. Quickly, he carried her outside into the fresh air and began shaking her shoulders and calling her name, "Fannie, Fannie, wake up! Please wake up."

His wife blinked her brown glazed eyes, then opened them up only to see a very distressed husband.

'What happened?" she asked.

"The washing machine motor went haywire, and you passed out! Fumes filled the porch and could've killed you," John bellowed.

"Well, I think I'm okay now," Fannie slowly whispered.

"No, get a drink of water and lay down for a little bit," he gently ordered.

And so she obeyed her husband for about an hour and rested her head against the cool pillow in their bedroom. Then she quickly sprung up and decided that because she felt better, she would resume the laundry. How else would all those clothes get washed? The only housekeepers she had were her daughters, and they were in school for most of the day.

Years later, the automatic washing machine replaced the conventional one. A suds saver recycled water into the cement washtub, then back into the machine. Whites were washed first in the hottest water which was saved and reused with each load. Ray's barn clothes were washed last and the gray foul-smelling water finally made its way down the drain, having been recycled several times.

All washed laundry was hung outside but in the coldest of winter, women resorted to stringing clotheslines in the basement. Throughout the day, children played hide-and-seek among the shirts and sheets which neatly hung from lines connected to the basement rafters. Eventually the invention of the clothes dryer revolutionized wash day. No longer an all day process, instead in an hour or two, all the clothes were laundered, dry and neatly put away in their rightful place.

Tuesday was ironing day. The ironing board was set up perpendicular to the living room wall, positioned so the TV could be viewed while pressing the clothes. Just about everything was ironed from sheets to undershirts. Permanent press fabrics weren't yet on the market. Consequently, the heavy iron sputtered and steamed as Millie's steady hand moved back and forth across the fabric. After Mom finished ironing, the little girl was asked to press pillowcases and her dad's hankies.

Television became a major part of the family's entertainment. Yet Ray's father, Ed, as well as many members of his church, believed that the TV and watching worldly programs were a sin. Contrary to Pa's opinion, Ray and Millie bought their first TV, a black-and-white Philco, in 1954. The antenna or rabbit ears needed to be adjusted every few minutes for better reception to the two Duluth television stations.

Ten years later, when upgrading their television, Lynn accompanied her parents to Carters, the local appliance store, to check out the new colored TVs. The salesman showed them several models arranged in an orderly fashion along the store's east wall. The Juntunens left with brochures in hand to study. Two days later, the little girl with crooked bangs and her mother returned to the store. Millie bought their very first RCA console colored television and wrote a check for $495 and signed it by writing Ray's name not hers. She often forged his name on checks or documents.

"Delivery could be the next day, Mrs. Juntunen," Jack Carter said, to which Lynn shouted, "Yes!"

A very jubilant daughter rode home with her mother. Before doing anything else, the little girl raced across the road to the farm to tell her father the good news.

"Dad, we got the TV, and it'll be delivered tomorrow!"

Ray grinned at his daughter and nodded. "Good, we can watch Bonanza on Sunday night."

When making major purchases like the TV or a new car, often, Ray included Lynn by asking her opinion. This consulting left her with a sense of ownership and confidence. She believed that her father valued her thoughts and feedback. Looking back, his "baby" received an enormous gift. He listened even though she was a child. The father made his daughter believe that her input was relevant. Clearly, Ray made his own decisions, even though he allowed his daughter to think that she was a factor in the outcome.

By the mid 60's, three stations broadcast out of Duluth. Each night, Lynn looked forward to sitting with her parents and watching many programs in "living color." The fifties and sixties were called "the Golden Age of Television," and Sunday nights were favorite nights because of the listings.

Sunday evening began at six o'clock with *Walt Disney's Wonderful World of Color*, followed by *Bonanza*, the story of Big Ben and his sons of the Ponderosa. Bob Bergstedt dubbed Ray "Big Ben of the Ponderosa." He did so because Ray and his brothers owned a "ranch" with over four hundred acres of prime real estate in the township. Ray was the big landowner like Ben Cartwright on Bonanza.

Other sitcoms namely *I Love Lucy* and *Andy Griffith Show* and game shows particularly *I've Got a Secret* and *What's My Line?* were weeknight favorites. Variety shows *The Ed Sullivan Show, The Perry Como Show*, and *Your Hit Parade* were followed by the local ten o'clock news with Earl Henton.

A trip to the town of Cloquet, to the bank, and to the grocery store was usually made on Friday.

Food was a very important part of the Finnish culture. Meals were family bonding times. Children were expected to sit around the table with their parents and enjoy the dishes that Mom prepared.

The little girl decided that Swanson frozen TV dinners, introduced in the '50s, were served only in homes where mothers worked outside of the home, did not know how to cook, or were just plain lazy.

Lynn knew it was wrong to be lazy but, like a typical child, still tried to get out of dishwashing and cleanup. Those tasks were delegated to the girls while the men and boys excused themselves from the table to relax so their food could "settle." At the time, the little girl thought it unfair, not knowing that soon changes in traditional male and female roles would be challenged by the Women's Liberation Movement.

Saturday was designated as cleaning day. The Electrolux was pulled out from the hall closet and rolled up and down across the floors. Sometimes, when Janet didn't feel too ambitious that day, she yanked the vacuum into her bedroom and shut the door. Then with motor running, she lay on the bed for several minutes. Mildred thought Janet was doing such a fine job thoroughly cleaning her room. Unbeknownst to her mother, Janet was sprawled out on the bed, reading a magazine.

The baby of the family got off much easier. Lynn's Saturday cleaning duty amounted to dusting furniture. Reluctantly, she grabbed the Pledge bottle and soft rag from underneath the kitchen sink and hurriedly stroked the oak end tables and coffee table. Then she ran through the three bedrooms one by one swirling dust around each room. Yet, when she returned to the piano, Lynn carefully removed her brother's eight-by-ten-inch framed graduation picture and studied it closely. She longed to better know him and didn't understand why he never visited his parents anymore.

Cartoons on Saturday mornings mesmerized Lynn from 7:00 a.m. through 9:00 a.m. After *Howdy Doody Time*, she licked raw dough from the beaters while her mom or sister baked chocolate chip cookies or pies for Sunday. The oven was never turned on for just one item. That was a wasteful use of electricity, according to Lynn's mother.

So after the desserts were baked, a Chef Boyardee pizza was assembled and placed in the oven on a cookie sheet. After thirty minutes, the buzzer went off, and lunch was ready. Every kid in America thought Chef Boyardee's pizza was the best meal since the advent of hamburgers. Lynn heartily ate the doughy pizza until her stomach ached and her sodium and gluten levels skyrocketed.

Before a sauna was built in the basement, Saturday night was sauna night at the Sunnarborg farm. The traditional Finnish bathing ritual was enjoyed by many of Lynn's cousins, aunts, and uncles. Moms and young children went first; men took sauna last.

Sunday morning's obligation meant Sunday school and church, followed at home with a more elaborate dinner. The meal always ended with a delicious dessert. Ray loved his desserts! Unlike today, most meals were prepared and eaten at home. Only on special occasions did the family go to a restaurant.

The Juntunens subscribed to the daily newspaper, the *Duluth Tribune*. But Sunday's paper was the family's favorite. While parents digested the editorials, obituaries, and local section, their children fought over the "funny papers." *Dennis the Menace*, *Blondie*, and *Hi and Lois* were Lynn's favorites, while Ray admitted to following *Dick Tracy* and *Rex Morgan*.

Sunday afternoons seemed endless if you were a kid and wanted to do something fun. After the big meal and dishes done, Lynn's parents excused themselves to their bedroom to take a little siesta, or that's what she was told. Years later, she concluded that they were having some "afternoon delight."

Later in the evening, the television became center stage.

Weeknights were reserved for visiting friends or extended family. During suppertime, the table conversation centered around whose turn it was to visit. Ray would lead the discussion.

"We were at the Kinnunens last time. Now it's their turn to come here. Why don't you call them up, Mildred? Or how about Lyytinens?"

Once the dishes were washed and put away, Mildred made the phone call either inviting people over or asking if they wanted company.

"Visiting" was very common among friends and family. Upon first arriving, guests sat in the living room discussing the local news, sports highlights, or the latest gossip. Then the hostess excused herself and made her way into the kitchen to prepare a small lunch. Always fresh hot coffee and a sweet dessert went along with the conversation.

Cigarettes were enjoyed by most adults, except Lynn's mother. These visitors filled the house with thick smoke. After the company left, Millie opened doors and windows for fresh air. Once again, the lady of the house was ahead of her time. No one understood the dangers of secondhand smoke, but Millie recognized that her nostrils burned, and her children should not breathe what bothered her nose.

During the '60s, basements were remodeled into rec (recreation) or family rooms. Ray and Mildred joined the movement to finish off their basement. Since Ray's good friend owned the local lumber company, all supplies were purchased from Ray "Kimpoo" Kinnunen and a plan outlined. He came over that evening to help his buddy Ray get started on the project.

The men nailed together a few two-by-fours making partition walls covered by eight-foot sheets of birch paneling. A Finnish bricklayer, Ericki Korpela, designed and erected the corner fireplace with matching woodbox and planter. Lynn thought the room was so beautiful. Dimming the lights, the girl built a roaring fire, and played records on the RCA portable stereo for hours on end. She crooned to songs by the Beatles, Everly Brothers, and Leslie Gore.

A used sleeper sofa, chair, and the old black-and-white television furnished the family room. The floor was tiled with linoleum squares, and scatter rugs surrounded the furniture. These spaces became the kids' hang out while their parents visited.

Young girls hosted pajama parties in the family rooms, and Lynn was no exception. She loved planning the sleepovers, inviting at least two or three friends at the beginning of the week. Throughout the following days, the girls chattered whenever possible about the anticipated fun. Once Friday came, all invitees carried to school small overnight cases which contained pj's, records of their favorite artists, as well as a sleeping bag.

When the school day was over, Lynn's friends paraded one by one onto bus 2. Each had a signed note from a parent giving permission to ride the bus to Lynn Juntunen's house. The wiggling, giggling girls squeezed into the overcrowded bus seats. Confidently, Lynn reassured them that there were only three stops before getting off at her house.

Sloppy joes, potato chips with sour cream dip, Fritos, and Cheetos were washed down with Coke or 7-Up. Later on, before bedtime, the girls snacked on brownies, Neapolitan ice cream and O'Henry bars, satisfying their sweet tooth.

They settled into the basement family room which, unfortunately, was located directly below the master bedroom. The hostess with her crooked bangs attempted to keep the noise level down. For young girls, that task was impossible. Still Mildred and Ray never complained about the loud voices or music. They understood that "kids will be kids."

Lynn used her Girl Scout skills to build a roaring fire in the brick corner fireplace and made certain the flue was open. Once she forgot and gray smoke billowed into the 14'x12' room, leaving a foul odor for days. Even so, she learned her lesson, and before long, a crackling fire warmed the room as flames licked over the dry birch logs.

For entertainment, the record player spun the newest 45s and albums. The girls sang the lyrics word for word. While dancing around the room, they watched each other to mimic the latest shimmy shake, twist, or hustle.

When the clock struck ten, everyone put on their jammies and slippers and then nestled into their sleeping bags. The plan was to stay awake all night long. In reality, the girls had a hard time keeping their eyes open long enough to see the end of Tarzan the late night feature on TV. Morning came all too soon, and phone calls were made for parents to pick up their very tired and slightly irritable daughters.

All in all, the little girl's household ran smoothly under the careful direction of the lady in charge, Millie. The daily routine created a cohesive environment. The family knew the plan and their role. Although the nightly news on TV showed wars, famine, and destruction, there was, for the most part, a peace within the walls of the little girl's home and she slept well every night except if thunder boomed and lightning flashed. Then she darted into her parent's bed.

CHAPTER 19

My Daddy, the Milkman, and the Farmer

The steps of a good man are ordered by the Lord. I have
been young and now I am old; yet I have not seen the
righteous forsaken or their descendants begging for bread.
—Psalm 37: 23, 25 (NKJV)

ALTHOUGH JOSEPH AND HIS WIFE bought the Mikola homestead in
1885, he and his sons, Edwin and Henry, did not begin delivering
Meadowbrook Dairy milk to grocery stores until 1919. As the years
passed, the eldest son Edwin took the reins and in 1939 bought out
his brother, Henry. It was Ed's good fortune that God blessed him
with many sons, who strove to establish Meadowbrook as the leading
supplier of milk products in all of Carlton County.

After World War 2, the country enjoyed postwar economic
prosperity. General Dwight D. Eisenhower was elected President and
the Juntunens chanted, "I like Ike!" The dairy business grew and was
unique as a family partnership of six brothers with their father, who
was the major decision-maker. They expanded their retail operations
and increased the herd by raising heifers.

Daddy's little girl shadowed him during the day whenever possible. Chores around the dairy farm repeated themselves daily. After

morning milking and breakfast, Ray picked up unprocessed milk in cans from local farmers and transported it back to the milk house to be pasteurized. Once in a while, Lynn begged to ride along with her dad to pick up the raw milk. When Ray agreed, the two would stop for coffee at several farms.

Together, they walked up the broken cement sidewalk to a yard filled with dandelions. They strolled onto the massive front porch and smelled the coffee and pine tar floors all at the same time. Usually, a cat scurried underneath the steps where chunks of cow manure stuck to one side.

Walking into the spacious country kitchen, Raymond proudly introduced his daughter to the farmer's wife, "Do you remember Lynn? She's our baby."

The woman acknowledged Lynn and offered a sweet pastry with a sweeter smile.

This introduction was standard for Lynn's dad, who said the words with such pride. The little girl never grew tired of hearing them. She felt special.

The farmer, his wife, Ray, and Lynn sat down at the big round table covered with a cotton linen tablecloth. The men slurped steamy cups of coffee and talked farming. Lynn looked around the unfamiliar kitchen, then back to the embroidered flowers along the edge of the tablecloth. There were times she had watched her mother use big metal hoops and stitch colored thread back and forth making similar designs. She decided the farmer's wife must know to do that, too. The little girl never forgot the warm hospitality shown around the table with the flowered tablecloth.

Returning to the processing plant, the raw milk was emptied from the milk cans, pasteurized, and filled into glass bottles or half-gallon cartons. Orange juice, butter, sour cream, and cottage cheese obtained from a wholesale distributor, offered the customers a full line of dairy products.

Willard was a whiz at math, and every day, he calculated how much milk would be needed for the next day's delivery. By 1956, Meadowbrook processed about two thousand quarts of milk daily. Three delivery trucks transported the dairy products to hundreds of homes and grocery stores on every day except Sunday. The only Sunday chore on the farm was milking the cows because it was a necessity. Otherwise, the Sabbath was to be kept holy, according to Ed Juntunen.

Back in the fifties and sixties, the milkman was entrusted to enter the house even when no one was home. He would place the "fresh milk" in the back of the refrigerator and slide the older milk to the front to be used first. If the customer was home when the milkman arrived at the door, often, he was invited into the kitchen for a cup of coffee and sometimes even breakfast. Yet well aware of his tight delivery schedule, the milkman quickly swallowed the hot coffee and went on to the next stop, repeating the morning custom again and again. By the time he completed his route, an antacid and a piss stop were necessary. Then once back at the dairy, he restocked the truck and walked to the farmhouse office to complete the daily paperwork.

Ed, the pious father, served as the business manager. He kept meticulous records of sales and expenditures and did the payroll all with only a fifth-grade education. Once Ray failed to report the $50 sale of a calf, and his father was not happy. He reminded Ray that with honesty God would bless the business in a greater way. Guess he was right.

As the moments became days and then years, Raymond and his five brothers, under the guidance of their father, expanded and updated Meadowbrook Dairy. The "boys" continued to buy property in Thomson Township. Improvements were made to the barn while the creamery doubled in size.

The quality of products and integrity of the family business proved valuable teaching tools for Lynn, her siblings, and cousins.

By 1967, the brothers formed a corporation, as Ed quietly ceased ownership. They worked harmoniously for the common good of the corporation, thus generating high dividends. There was great pride with providing a top-quality product for a demanding market. This was Lynn's first glimpse of the free enterprise system, alive and well in America.

Each of the "boys" was entrusted with a different facet of farm operations. At Meadowbrook, "we" was the operative pronoun, not "I." What was best for the business, not what was best for me, became the unselfish family creed. The six brothers, Edwin, Raymond, Willard, Howard, Wally, and Wilbur had few differences. Yet there came a time in the seventies when Willy, whom the children referred to as Billy, decided to leave the corporation. His brothers wished him well when he bought a small fuel oil business. Unfortunately, the oil embargo was imposed on the United States by Arab members of the Organization of Petroleum Exporting Countries. OPEC elevated the price and the availability of crude oil. This series of events jeopardized any oil company but especially a fledgling business.

Back at the dairy, now there were five. The brothers hired an additional employee to help fill in the gaps. Days off and vacation times were equally distributed among the brothers.

Yet, one brother rarely took a day off. Every morning, Willard faithfully woke up before 3:00 a.m. and walked from his house about 250 yards over to the milk house. Once there, he set the coffee to brew and began his day calculating how much milk to bottle based on sales from the day before.

Making buttermilk was particularly difficult as raw milk had to be free of antibiotics. Only cows that had not been treated for mastitis qualified to give milk for making buttermilk. Also, it was imperative that the culture be timed perfectly. Only Willard knew and understood this process completely.

The once small dairy farm that sold milk from a horse-drawn wagon was deemed the leading dairy farm in Carlton County one hundred years later. Wholesale and retail routes crisscrossed Cloquet, Scanlon, and Esko. Painted on the side of the four cream colored milk trucks was the slogan 'Meadowbrook Dairy---You can't beat our milk, but you can whip our cream.'

Even Orthodox Jews from Minneapolis picked up milk from the dairy. Four times a year, a rabbi with his entourage personally came to the barn and prayed while the cows were being milked. Full-bearded, he entered the milking parlor wearing the traditional black floor-length cassock. Headwear included his kippah over which he wore a *borsalino* hat and black dress shoes. Ray secretly wondered if the rabbi was uncomfortable in his clergy attire and decided he must stink to high heaven after leaving the barn.

The next day, after the milk was pasteurized, the rabbi returned with a small trailer and hauled cases of Kosher milk back to the metro area. Some of the milk was sold in Duluth, but the majority was frozen in cartons for easier shipment to the Twin Cities.

Ray respected the beliefs and traditions of the Jewish rabbi; he respected his father and the dairy business that he and his brothers operated. Though most of all, others respected Ray as a good man and caring father. A favorite ending to each day was when his little girl nestled close to her daddy as he told bedtime stories.

He lay flat on his back stretched out with rounded chest facing the ceiling. His body so large in the bed and his very presence larger, he made his youngest daughter feel truly safe.

His unique fables with vivid imagery kept the child spellbound. Most of the stories were ones Ray fabricated with the characters becoming talking animals. One favorite bedtime story was about a baby bear who lost his way in the deep dark woods. All alone and afraid, the cub spoke to Ray, pleading for directions back to his den. Ray became a character in many of his stories, and the animals talked to him. The little bear couldn't find his mother. He was cold, hungry, afraid, and crying.

At about this point, Ray would sniffle and pretend to cry like he was the little lost bear. Identifying with baby bear's fearful situation, Lynn burst into tears. Quickly, the story line developed to become brighter, and the lost cub found his way home. Always there was a happy ending.

Singing tales were also a part of Ray's repertoire, and his children begged for him to sing the woeful tune about a sad horse whose rider had died.

"There's an empty cot in the bunkhouse tonight. Old Paint's head hanging low. His spurs an' chaps hang on the wall, Limpey's gone where the good cowboys go," crooned Ray.

The song told of loss, which, in life, inevitably occurs. He hoped his young listeners showed signs of remorse or sadness, and he wanted their hearts to learn about compassion and sympathy.

Resting in her father's arms, Lynn Rae listened attentively to these make-believe stories and songs. The bedtime ritual provided great comfort and a sense of security and protection. She believed that her father would be present in moments of good times and difficult times. This belief was a precursor to Lynn understanding the loving Heavenly Father's arms as they safely protected her in times of fear and danger.

CHAPTER 20

Prayer

The Spirit helps us in our weakness; for we do
not know how to pray, but the Spirit himself
intercedes with groanings too deep for words.
—Romans 8:26 (NASB)

FAMILIES WERE MEANT TO BE *a support system for one another. A group can fight off an enemy easier than one. The once "little girl with the crooked bangs" needed all of her family and friends to pray. Her life was in jeopardy, and she needed help.*

From Miami to New York to California intercession was made on Lynn's behalf. Prayer chains were activated, and hundreds, even complete strangers, called out to God to heal the woman who was hit head-on in a motor vehicle accident.

When the family got to the hospital, Russ saw Lynn being taken on a gurney for a CAT scan. She pulled at her hair and talked gibberish. Later, she told the family that she remembered fervently praying because she sensed something was very wrong. Yet at that moment no one knew what she was doing or what was happening to her.

At first glance, the doctor thought a clot from the broken femur had passed somewhere through the brain, restricting blood flow.

Russ's heart cracked open, and the family's emotions sunk deeply into an abyss. Just yesterday, everyone had been encouraged by Lynn's transfer from intensive care to the fourth floor. Their hopes banished with the diagnosis that her symptoms indicated she had a stroke. Yet the results of the scan showed no sign of a clot. This complicated matters. If a clot from the broken femur had been discovered, a blood thinner may have dissolved it. Consequently, more blood work was ordered, as well as an EEG to analyze electrical activity within Lynn's brain.

After these procedures were completed, the neurologist came back to the unit. He took Russ over to the side and privately explained that the damage to Lynn's brain might be irreversible. Her cognitive and motor skills may be compromised. It was more than this husband could comprehend.

Russ slowly walked back into the ICU and checked on his wife. She wasn't pulling at her matted hair anymore but was still. Russ felt sick. He wanted to find a bathroom where he could throw up. Lynn stared ahead blankly and did not respond to his voice.

Sadly, he trudged down the hospital hallway to the waiting area where his daughters held vigil. Amy and Brooke mindlessly thumbed through the well-worn magazines, while Robyn lay recoiled on the green vinyl couch. Minutes earlier, Janet arrived with Russ's mother, Jackie. The two women sat together, whispering when Russ entered. He looked around the room and wondered how he would tell his daughters the neurologist's findings.

What would he say? How could he tell them that their mother may remain in a vegetative state? How could he explain that she may never talk to them again? Smile again? Know who they are?

Earlier in the day, Janet printed Bible verses onto three index cards for her three nieces. Robyn, Brooke, and Amy often reached into their pockets to retrieve the little cards with the powerful words. The girls referred to them again and again, claiming the healing scriptures for their mother. Now more than ever, they needed God's intervention.

As if on cue, Chaplain Joan appeared just as Russ was about to open his mouth. He looked over to her and asked, "Could you pray for Lynn? For us?"

"Yes, of course!" Joan replied and led them in the most beautiful prayer of healing for this woman they so dearly loved and for each one of them. For they were weary and their hearts were weighed down with unrelenting sadness.

Tears flowed from their tired eyes, and hugs were shared among the group. Surprisingly, they felt better and noticed Aunt Patty enter the family waiting room. She carried in her arms a large white box filled with chocolate-frosted brownies, freshly baked that morning. Nothing says love like chocolate. Everyone sampled the delectable goodies and were soothed by Patty's gift of compassion and love.

Swimming hole bridge on the Midway River

Joseph and Elsa (Pykkonen) Juntunen

Wedding picture of John and Fannie (Carlson) Sunnarborg

Frederick and Mary (Holm) Carlson

John and Fannie Sunnarborg Family
Sitting right to left : Lorraine "Lola", Fannie, John, Betsy
Middle row: Mildred, Alice, Martin, Doris, Clarence, Gladys
Back row: Lloyd, Fred, Kenneth, Johnny

Young Ray with Percherons

Esther Sjoblad and A. Edwin Juntunen

Aerial view of Meadowbrook Dairy in 1952

Andrew Edwin and Esther (Sjoblad) Juntunen Family
Seated left to right: Doris "Dottie", Edwin,
Esther, Ed. Sr, Bernice, Marion
Standing: Verna, Howard, Willard, Raymond, Carol,
Allen, Wilbur, Wallace, Barbara, Thomas

Flower Girl

Lynn and her sister Janet

Kindergarten Teeny Weeny Band

Miss Meadowbrook Parade

The Circus is Here and a Calf

Wedding October 1971

Cheerleaders in 1969 left to right Mary, Vicki,
Marion, Connie, Judy, Lynn

Christmas 1982

Bridal photo of Mildred 9-18-40

Millie and Ray   50th anniversary

Family left to right: Jack, Matt, Brooke, Nolan, Russ, Lynn,
Max, Nate, Amy, Peter, Sam, Robyn, Sophia, & Steve
Courtesy of Shelley Robideaux Photography

Six grandchildren: standing left to right Nathaniel,
Nolan, Jackson, Samuel, and Maxwell.
Sitting: Gramma Lynn and Sophia

Courtesy of Shelley Robideaux Photography

Our family: standing left to right Robyn, Sam, Steve, Russ, Matt, Brooke, Peter, Amy, Nolan
Sitting left to right Max, Sophia, Lynn, Jack, Nate
Courtesy of Shelley Robideaux Photography

CHAPTER 21

The Seasons of Life

The wind blows wherever it pleases. You hear its sound,
but you cannot tell where it comes from or where it is
going. So it is with everyone who is born of the Spirit.

—John 3:8 (NIV)

FEW CAN BOAST OF HAVING seventy-one first cousins. The little girl just took for granted and assumed that everyone's family was similar to hers. Cousins were her first friends, her forever friends.

During summer vacation, eight of Lynn's paternal first cousins were together just about every day. The seven girls and one boy were neighbors, as well as playmates. Their entertainment included softball, croquet, and H-O-R-S-E; and after supper when their dads were done working, they played hide-and-seek at the farm.

Their creative sides emerged by directing grand productions. Shortly after watching the Miss America Pageant on TV, the cousins decided to host a contest to choose their own queen, Miss Meadowbrook, named appropriately for the dairy. The pageant followed a similar format to the Miss America competition. Contestants were judged from three categories: evening gown, swimsuit, and talent. The five candidates practiced walking in their plastic high heels, singing or dancing, as well as strutting across the stage in their favorite swimsuits. Two aunts, Kathy B. and Verna, were the unbiased judges, having no children in the competition. After careful tabulating, the master of ceremonies, Bob "Warren" Barker, announced that Lisa was selected Miss Meadowbrook. Everyone cheered, and a parade ensued with the queen and two princesses sitting atop the "float," a red wagon decorated with Kleenex carnations.

As soon as the pageant concluded, the cousins moved on to summer theater. This endeavor required days of planning and preparation. Reluctantly, Lynn's parents relinquished their garage for several days while the troupe rehearsed. Chairs were set up on one side and a curtain and stage on the other side. Sometimes, the children argued about the format, stage props, and musical selections. If the planning sessions became too heated, the oldest cousin, Patsy, would arbitrate and make the final call. She was fair and respected, hence arguing ceased for a while.

Early on, a pecking order was established. The three youngest cousins went along with whatever they were told. They were called "the little kids." The others were caught in the middle. Whoever was the loudest or most convincing survived at least for the moment.

The moms and neighbors were invited to every performance. Ticket sales were conducted in advance, so the stage crew knew how many chairs to set up on opening day.

One summer *The Four Seasons* play was created. The group performed songs and skits depicting each season of the year. Springtime brought showers with three actors twirling umbrellas as they warbled Bing Crosby's hit "Singing in the Rain." Act II, summer, gave way to swimsuits and Hula-Hoops.

Later, the group came up with the brilliant idea to have falling snowflakes as a perfect prop for a winter scene. Or so the crew thought. But that turned out to be quite a fiasco!

First, thousands of pieces of white paper were cut into confetti snowflakes and stuffed into an old leather purse for safekeeping. Then it was determined that somebody needed to get to the attic to disperse the falling snow. After much debate, a decision was made before the winter segment began, there'd be a commercial about a gas station, since one was currently running fifteen second spots on nightly TV. The advertisement involved service attendants climbing a ladder. Accordingly, a ladder was lifted to the garage rafters.

Then four actors chanted "Super Saver! Super Saver!" drawing the audience's attention to them instead of the one slithering up the ladder, escaping to the attic.

On the day of the performance, everyone was excited for the 1:00 p.m. curtain to rise. The actors had their final dress rehearsal that morning. After a quick lunch, the thespians rushed back to the garage to await the arrival of their audience.

Earlier, it was decided that the winter scene should be the last act since the confetti snow would be strewn everywhere. The curtain opened to the season of spring with tulips, umbrellas, and Bing Crosby's song. Summer followed with girls in bright swimsuits romping by the sandy beach. The season of autumn came next. Each sketch proceeded without a hitch until the last act of winter.

The Super Saver gas station commercial allowed Lynn to escape to the garage attic. Then the three "little kids," took the stage bundled in heavy woolen coats, mittens, long scarves, and boots. Together they sang the familiar tune "Frosty the Snowman" with the finale being the wintery favorite "Let it Snow." The time came near the end of the song for snow to gently fall down from the sky. Teetering from the trusses, Lynn shook white paper "snowflakes" from the soft leather purse.

Unfortunately, she got caught up in the moment and lost control of the purse. It fell out of her hand unto the stage floor with a thud. Lynn looked down in horror at Warren, the MC. He burst out in laughter, as did everyone else.

Fortunately, there was only one performance. Once the production ended, the cousins swept the confetti snow from garage floor, returned the folding chairs to their rightful homes, and moved on to another project.

When the winter months arrived, the young cousins transferred their energies from summer productions to snow forts. After a fresh dumping of snow, Ray plowed the farmyard and family driveways. He pushed drifts with the John Deere tractor and loader and intentionally made high banks, perfect for building massive forts. The kids tunneled with shovels and pawed with their mittened hands into the clean white mounds, making rooms and barricades.

Because the girls outnumbered the one boy cousin, snowball fights rarely occurred. Instead, they preferred creating "houses in the snow," not war zones. The interior of the cave was soundproof except occasionally boots could be heard crunching across the snowy roof-top. Once the cave was completed, the children took time to slide down the slippery slope on aluminum flying saucers.

A playhouse that great-uncle Henry built twenty-five years ear-lier was moved from his former yard to behind the fencing of the little girl's house. Once in its new location, Ray and his brothers secured the 10' x 14' floor of the structure to railroad ties. With a little elbow grease Lynn and her Meadowbrook cousins scrubbed the wood floor and painted the trim and base boards a sunny, bright yellow. Mother picked up several outdated wallpaper books from the paint store. A paste of flour and water was slathered onto the backs of the samples and a plumb line determined an accurate vertical. One at a time, the wallpaper pieces were pasted to the walls, creating a multi-colored design, then rubbed with old rags, over and over until the air bubbles disappeared. The interior walls became like grandmother's patchwork quilt. Furnishings included old milk crates, a small table, stools, and a large scatter rug. Two window valances were sewed from old drapery material. Grass around the building was mowed and a small flower bed was planted under the window.

Once or twice during the summer, the girls slept overnight in sleeping bags on the floor. After the sun set across the Midway, dark-ness filled up the night sky.

"Let there be light!" the girls shouted in unison as their flash-lights transformed the playhouse interior to a soft yellow glow. As expected, the flashlights made their way to the girls' chins, shining straight up to reveal scary mouths that narrated scary stories. Ghosts and games and giggles entertained for an hour or two. Yet, it had been a long day preparing for the playhouse over-nighter, and soon the girls grew quiet. All that was heard was the sudden slap of skin con-firming the demise of a buzzing mosquito. When the morning light filtered through the window panes, one by one the girls sleepily trod-ded back to their respective homes. They crawled into warm, comfy beds and slept for another hour or two in their bug-free bedrooms.

The cousins were always encouraged to play outside to get fresh air. They embraced their Sami ancestry unaware that they were mimicking these indigenous relatives in several ways. Between summer and winter, there was plenty of time to roam deep in the woods behind Lynn's house, exploring the narrow road leading to the pigpen.

Purple violets were discovered in May amongst the shade of the poplar, while strawberry plants were left to bloom and ripen until late June. Wild raspberry bushes hugged the rock piles along the fence line. Beyond the trees and higher ground, the swamps were speckled with yellow cowslips often called marsh marigolds. Lynn always picked a bouquet before going home.

"Mom, Mom! Look what I found in the woods!" the little girl announced.

"Oh, they are beautiful!" Mom praised the child while arranging the flowers into a jelly jar vase.

"I picked some more and put them in our fort near the pigpen too."

The original fort, eight feet above ground, was first constructed by Big Brother and refurbished ten years later by Lynn and the neighboring cousins. A triangular platform fitted between three trees was built from scrap boards scavenged from garages or sheds. After the fort was done, the kids climbed from the makeshift ladder onto the platform. Using drums made from Quaker Oats boxes and old tin cans, they beat and chanted until their palms ached and their voices grew hoarse. They called the tree platform their "tom-tom fort" for the native beating of the drums.

Later, when the cousins grew tired of the tom-tom fort, a much different structure was built deeper in the woods, designed similar to a teepee hut with long twelve-foot poles meeting in the center. Binder twine laced the top of the poles securely together. First, larger sticks, then twigs were horizontally threaded between the poles. Lastly, evergreen boughs were skillfully woven on top of the sticks to seal out any of the elements. A small 3'x3' opening served as the door. Kelly green moss carpeted the teepee floor, making it soft and cushy. Carefully selected rocks surrounded the yard with paths intersecting from each direction. The cousins were convinced that the teepee fort was a monumental achievement.

The forest was remarkably spiritual. Indigenous natives understood this concept by respecting nature and the land they'd been given. The little girl loved the land too. Joseph Juntunen, her great-grandfather, had acquired this acreage a long time ago; still she felt an ownership to this hallowed ground.

She wondered if her cousins felt the same way but never asked. Instead, she often walked by herself to the tee-pee fort and one day experienced an unusual phenomenon.

Sunday afternoons were long and boring to a ten-year-old. Just what could she do to pass the time from 1:00 p.m. until supper? No television shows appealed to her, the Sunday "funny papers" read. So Lynn decided to take a walk to the teepee fort.

The brilliant May sun glided down through the tree branches as Lynn made her way along the well-worn path. There was a stillness in the forest except an occasional rustle of leaves when a gray squirrel dashed across a limb.

The little girl looked up and smiled. Both the squirrel and she were happy that the snow had finally melted and they could rummage around the tree trunks.

When Lynn got to the teepee, she assessed it for any winter damage. A stick or two had broken loose, but, overall, the fort remained undisturbed. The child shifted her leg slightly and entered the teepee. Thick green moss, which blanketed the tent floor, was slightly damp. The frost had finally lifted from beneath the ground.

Lynn sat down on the log stool, sighed, and took in the moment. Her roving eyes, moving from side to side, studied the structure. It was a remarkable accomplishment she decided and wished Warren was there so, together, the two could admire their craftsmanship. She inhaled deeply, and the scent from the spruce boughs filled her tiny nostrils. Slowly, she got up and bent low to exit the fort.

Once outside, she looked up. The treetops gently swayed high above, and she heard the wind song flowing through the spruce needles. Yet surprisingly there was a stillness on the forest floor.

The little girl kept looking up as the sun's rays filtered downward. She sensed that she was not alone. Still Lynn knew no one followed her to the teepee fort. The whispering wind continued, and all at once, she understood. The God of Creation was there with her. She couldn't rationalize or explain, but she knew that she sensed God's Spirit, and it was very restorative.

Lynn never mentioned to anyone her experience in the woods that day, nor did she obsess about it. Who would believe her anyway? She was just a little girl playing among the trees in the forest.

CHAPTER 22

Five Year Sisters

Because I rescued the poor who cried for help,
And the orphan who had no helper.
—Job 29:12 (NRSV)

ON TWO SEPARATE OCCASIONS DURING the mid-forties and again in the late fifties, Ray and Mildred opened their home to a niece. The young girls unexpectedly lost at least one parent to a tragic death and they needed a stable environment. Mother's strong broad shoulders attempted to carry the burden for her nieces. Grief counseling was not yet available. Yet the girls desperately needed outside intervention.

Kathy came to live with Janet, Rod, Mildred, and Ray after her twenty-year-old mother Shirley died in 1945. No autopsy was performed, yet the death certificate listed the cause as "internal bleeding," most likely an aneurysm. Ray's brother Howard plunged deep into grief, and his world shattered when his wife passed away. He was unable to both work at the farm and watch a toddler. So Mildred and Ray cared for Kathy, while Howard stayed with his parents in the large farmhouse next door and visited his daughter often.

Kathy was a beautiful child with dark curls and big brown eyes. She was seven months older than Janet. Mildred sewed matching frocks for the girls. People unknowingly believed they were twins.

Brother Rodney was three years older than the girls. The household was active with three children under the age of four.

Since Kathy was only a few months old when her biological mother died, no maternal bond developed between the two. Instead, Millie became the child's nurturing figure for five years. The little girl was kept busy playing with her "twin" Janet while Millie kept busy with sewing, laundry, and ironing. Since permanent press fabrics were nonexistent, everything laundered in the conventional washer and dried on a clothesline needed ironing. She starched and painstakingly pressed the girls' little dresses. Washing cloth diapers for two babies appeared endless, but Mildred never complained. Instead she took action, and before their second birthdays both girls were potty trained and the diapers were recycled into perfect cleaning rags. Out of necessity the captain ran a tight ship but was weary after the little skippers hit their bunks.

Soon a reprieve occurred when Howard remarried in 1950. Kathy left Ray's and Mildred's house, and her "sister and brother" and moved back with her biological father and her stepmother, Inga. The transition must have been a huge adjustment for both the six-year-old and for a young wife, who immediately assumed the role of mother to Kathy.

Twelve years later, Lynn and Janet acquired another "sister." Patsy stayed with Ray and Mildred for five years. Her father's body was discovered in the attic of their rented house in Duluth's Lincoln Park. One of the sisters spotted her dad's limp body hanging by a belt from the rafters. Patsy's younger sister claimed she saw the shadow of a person slipping out of the dark attic. Several of Johnny's children believed their dad was murdered because he owed money to the Duluth Mafia. The crime scene was quickly and perhaps carelessly investigated. Police reports stated that John Sunnarborg committed suicide. Those findings were never questioned, nor was a child's account given much credibility. Unfortunately, Johnny's wife Esther passed away shortly thereafter.

Because Johnny and his wife died without a will, eight underage children became wards of the state. Some went to live with relatives, while others were put up for adoption. Their household had been very dysfunctional, and alcoholism was a key factor in the parents' deaths.

Talking about the deaths may have helped considerably when coping with the breakup of Patsy's family. Instead, the children only heard adults whisper in hushed tones about their father and mother. Because it was believed that Johnny took his own life and since alcoholism was not treated as an illness, this death was perhaps misunderstood by the Sunnarborg family.

Patsy, the second daughter of Johnny and Esther, was bright, ambitious, and creative. Her siblings scattered and their lives shattered, the young girl needed a stable, balanced environment. As a result, she called Mildred and Ray her mom and dad and fit quite well into the family unit for over four years. Until the arguing began.

Granted this an oxymoron, Patsy was a credible peacemaker among the children. When she came into the Juntunen family, she automatically assumed the role of the cousins' mediator. She acted as negotiator and if necessary helped resolve most differences. All of the cousins respected her authority and listened when she advised as she was the eldest of the eight neighboring cousins.

However, with adolescence, peace passed over and Patsy became indignant, filled with suppressed anger. Her parents' death and the breakup of the immediate family left her harboring a wounded spirit. She quarreled with Lynn, Janet, and Mildred. Even Ray could not reason with her. Children's grief counseling was not available at the time.

Sadly, by the age of fourteen, Patsy left the Juntunens to live with Johnny's youngest sister Betsy and her husband. The household was a blend of families as well that consisted of two biological children and two grief-stricken nephews, whose parents drowned several years earlier near Puget Sound.

Everyone accepted the situation as best they could. Betsy worked tirelessly trying to manage the household and her husband's business dealings. Much like her mother, she never complained, instead found joy in her blended family.

The intense loss the "five-year sisters" experienced was never addressed. Years ago when a death occurred, the family buried their emotions right along with the casket. Talking about the deceased rarely occurred. Needless to say, as adult women, both "five-year sisters" had an emptiness in their hearts no one could fill. Their wounds, which never properly healed, were reflective by their choice of husbands, who were controlling and abusive. All the while, these two women yearned for the love, acceptance, and stability that they first saw modeled in Raymond.

CHAPTER 23

Performing

Sing to the Lord a new song, his praise in the assembly.
Let them praise his name with dancing.
—Psalm 149:1,3 (NIV)

THE LITTLE GIRL'S THEATRICAL INTERESTS heightened when at four years old, she appeared in a community play. Her mother cajoled both a reluctant husband and youngest child into acting in the comedy "It's Cold in Them Thar Hills." Lynn was cast as a Hillbilly child and consequently fell in love with the stage and performing for an audience.

Early on sister Janet acted as Lynn's first director. When nature called Janet into the bathroom for a bowel movement, she'd call out to Lynn, "Rehearsal time, come to the bathroom!"

Lickety-split the little girl slid sideways down the narrow linoleum hallway stopping abruptly at the bathroom door. The older sister handed her a Ban roll-on deodorant bottle, invented the year Lynn was born, which ingeniously became a microphone. As she balanced herself on the edge of the bathtub, Lynn crooned into the "mike" learning the melody and lyrics to many of the most popular songs on the radio.

On evenings, when "company" stopped by to visit her parents, Lynn discovered an audience. The rehearsed Top Ten hits from the radio would become her repertoire. "Let Me Go, Lover" was a favorite request. Lynn sang at the top of her lungs, using dramatic gestures for effectiveness. She relished all the attention.

Just a few years later, Lynn would try to duplicate those moments but, instead, was scolded for showing off. This turnaround confused the little girl because at one time her singing was acceptable. Now, it was frowned upon. Hence, Janet came to the rescue.

The two sisters re-enacted a popular daytime television show, "Queen for a Day" from once again, the bathroom. When Janet was taking a potty break, she called out the familiar opening question asked by the host, "Would you like to be queen for a day?" Once Lynn heard those words, she stopped whatever she was doing and ran into the bathroom.

The premise for the game show hedged on who could deliver the most convincing tragic story of their life. After hearing five contestants, a panel voted, and one woman was chosen by the studio audience as "queen" for that particular day. The queen was awarded many prizes to help her cope with her difficulties.

Each time the sisters played the bathroom game, Lynn impersonated a downtrodden contestant, while Janet became the moderator. Speaking into the pretend microphone, the contestant spun this incredibly sad yarn about her life, all the while the MC asked leading questions. Of course, Lynn won the contest and was crowned "Queen for a Day" and soon discovered that even toilet duties could be transformed into a creative game...no iPod or iPhone required. She never quite understood why her sister wanted an audience when she was taking a dump. But she did understand that it became yet another opportunity to perform.

Lynn's brother, Rodney, was having his moments as a king, as well. The six-foot-three teenager was a starting forward on the high school varsity basketball team. Hundreds of screaming fans packed the tiny Lincoln gym to watch their hometown boys win game after game.

Watching high school athletics was the major form of winter entertainment in the little community. Just about everyone attended the basketball games. A winning tradition was deeply embedded into the fabric of the school system and the town.

Children of all ages chanted, "Minneapolis and St. Paul, teeny-weeny Esko beats them all."

The small country bumpkins were pitted against the big-city slickers, and the local radio announcer predicted, "It's gonna be a barn burner tonight!"

Esko's enrollment was seventy-five percent less than the metro schools. Class sizes fluctuated between fifty to sixty students per grade. Yet against all odds, sometimes the small town team was victorious. A David vs. Goliath factor ensued, and the press loved it, splashing photos and articles across the sports pages. Year after year, Esko athletes stepped into the winner's circle holding championship trophies high over their heads. A winning tradition was firmly planted in the hearts of every Eskomo.

During his senior year, brother Rodney was courted by several colleges offering athletic scholarships. He and his cousin David were the stars of the basketball team. Along with the team's success, both boys were "the big men on campus."

At the same time, sister Janet hoped to be a member of the cheerleading B squad. In preparation for the tryouts, she practiced diligently the jumps, splits, and motions to the cheers. The living room picture window became her mirror to review and critique her reflection.

All at once, Janet had the fantastic idea to invite some girls to her house for a group practice session.

"Hey, Susie, why don't you and Carol come over after school?" Janet asked, "We could practice for tryouts."

"Sounds like a great idea, Jan. I'll ask Carol if she wants to join us."

After school six teenage girls jumped and cheered and laughed in the Juntunen's living room. After they left, Janet soaked in the hot bathtub. Her muscles were sore, and she wondered when there was a time that she didn't ache.

The next day were tryouts. All the girls who'd been practicing together the night before made the squad except Janet. She was the organizer and she cheered for all the others. Because Jan was such a good teacher, not only did her friends make the cheerleading squad;

her little sister watched and learned the words and motions to every cheer too.

Faithfully the little girl, along with her family, attended every Esko basketball game both at home and away. During one of the games, four-year-old Lynn was spotted among the euphoric crowd, jumping and following the arm movements of the cheerleaders.

Later that week, head cheerleader Marlene asked, "Janet, does Lynn know every cheer?"

"Yes, she does and the words to the school song too," bragged Janet.

The next day, the A team pep squad lobbied for a little Eskomo mascot and Lynn got the job. She filled the position for two years when she was four and five years old.

Millie sewed a royal blue pleated skirt with matching panties. A three-inch gold *E* was hand-stitched onto a white sweater. Saddle shoes were purchased that matched the cheerleaders' footwear. Lynn was invited to practice after school with the girls. Before the game, they presented her with her very own miniature pom-poms.

Marlene was a neighbor and family friend, who helped Lynn master one specific cheer that she was to do all by herself. The four-year-old skipped to the center of the gym floor, saying, "Ready O, let's go!"

Then she ran diagonally across the playing floor, did a cartwheel, followed by the splits, yelling, "Ooooo, boom, ahhhhh!"

She circled with her arms while chanting, "Esko High School, Rah! Rah! Rah!"

The fans loved the cheer and wildly applauded.

During one basketball game, there was a timeout.

Marlene told Lynn, "Okay, go out there and do your cheer."

Most floor cheers were done between these breaks, when coaches instructed the team in a huddle near their bench. The buzzer sounded when play resumed.

On that fateful day in February, the little cheerleader met her Waterloo. The referee blew the whistle, but the cheer wasn't over. Lynn was caught in the middle of the floor surrounded by giant basketball players towering over her. They stood around the center circle getting ready for the tip-off. Lynn looked up petrified and tried to edge her way back to the sidelines. At the last moment, she was able to thread through the boys' legs and quickly darted off the floor.

After that incident, she never wanted to go out to the center of the gym floor and do that cheer all by herself. The cheerleaders tried to coax her. For some reason, she just could not tell them her fears of being mauled by ten basketball players.

Perhaps *pride* was beginning to rear its ugly head at the early age of four? Needless to say, Lynn continued cheering with the A-squad. She never cried. She never appeared shaken. She never told anyone just how traumatized she was that fateful night. Lynn just continued to fulfill her role as the little Eskomo mascot. After all, she was in the limelight and loved every minute of it.

Millie and Ray were quite proud to have their son, a star basketball player, and their youngest daughter, the mascot cheerleader, together performing for the biggest show in town. Basketball was king in the Northland, and the community of Esko wholeheartedly supported their team.

The gymnasium on game nights was packed with hot, sweaty fans. The band played on as the majorettes performed at halftime. The local radio station broadcasted play-by-play action, while some of the men quietly bet on the game's outcome. It was the place to be on a Friday night. But the glory days soon ended.

Once Marlene and her cheering squad graduated from high school, a decision was made. Lynn was too old to be a mascot. She graduated from kindergarten and was attending first grade. Her little cheerleader days were history. However, the experience birthed in Lynn the confidence to lead a crowd and to perform in front of that crowd…great lessons at a young age. Reluctantly, she entered cheerleader semiretirement. Her moments as a varsity pepster would be resurrected ten years later at dear old Esko High.

Chapter 24

Only the Beginning

For it is God who is at work in you, both to
will and to work for His good pleasure.
—Philippians 2:13 (NASB)

SCHOOL DAYS FOR LYNN USHERED in Esko's first kindergarten class. Her sister and brother did not attend kindergarten since it was not offered before 1957. They began their elementary experience in first grade at the Washington School. Educators believed that kindergarten would be a head start for reading, writing, and arithmetic, yet more social and less structured than first grade.

Students had the option of attending a half-day session either in the morning or afternoon. Lynn was assigned to the morning class. She was happy because five cousins were also in her class. Furthermore, she still needed an afternoon nap. The rigorous morning schedule and later bedtimes after basketball games exhausted her.

By having five cousins as a support system, Lynn had no ambivalence starting school. She was not frightened or lonely, as in Ray's bedtime story about the lost little bear.

Lynn and her cousins played together almost every day, either at the dairy farm, where their dads worked or at the Sunnarborg's farm about two miles away, where her mother's parents lived.

On the first day of classes, five familiar little bodies were right beside Lynn for finger painting, milk, music, and rest time.

During the midmorning break, a snack of graham crackers and milk was furnished to the student. Everyone sat down in short-legged chairs spaced evenly along a Formica table. Lynn usually sat by Patti Nan. Although both of their last names began with *J*, Lynn claimed a far greater rationale. Believe it or not, Lynn disliked milk. Her family had access to an abundant supply of farm fresh dairy milk. Yet, with every swallow her stomach rolled. No doubt she was lactose intolerant, but that phrase was not yet in her vernacular. Lynn feared being scolded for not drinking her little carton of milk. Quickly, she discovered that her classmate Patti Nan loved milk and agreed to drink any or all of the little girl's. Every morning before class began, Lynn looked for Patti Nan, who thankfully that year had perfect attendance.

One morning during music time, Mrs. Gustafson, the teacher, passed out the silver triangles, wooden sticks, drums, and horns. Everyone took turns playing a different instrument while the teacher accompanied them on the piano.

A week before the Spring Concert, the teacher handed each pupil an instrument, except Lynn. Instead, Mrs. Gustafson walked over to the music stand. *Click, click* went her shoes on the caramel-colored pine floor. Nervously, Lynn looked up to see the matronly woman bend down.

She presented the little girl with a twelve-inch white baton. *Click, click* she tapped it on the music stand and announced, "You are going to be our director. Just wave the baton back and forth. You will lead our Teeny Weeny Band."

Lynn couldn't wait for the morning to end and get home to tell her mother the good news. Mom was always there waiting for her daughter to jump off the bus and run down the driveway into the house. Usually, Ray walked home a few minutes later. Lynn loved eating lunch with both parents.

She bubbled over with the good news. "Guess what?"

Yet before either of them could answer, Lynn blurted, "I've been picked to lead the kindergarten band at the spring program!"

Ray winked at his wife and continued eating his roast beef sandwich as Lynn chattered on with excitement.

Later in the afternoon, Mildred received a telephone call from Mrs. Gustafson.

"Hello, Mrs. Juntunen, this is Minette Gustafson. I'm certain Lynn has already told you that I've selected her to be the leader of our Kindergarten Teeny Weeny Band."

"Yes, she's pretty excited about that," Mildred replied.

Mrs. Gustafson continued, "Do you think you could sew a uniform for Lynn?"

"Of course, I can try. Do you have a particular style in mind?"

"I think something close to what a drum majorette wears would be suitable. Just use your imagination, Mrs. Juntunen. I'm certain whatever you make will be just fine."

"Thank you for calling, Mrs. Gustafson. I'll get right on it."

So it was that once again, Millie sat at her Singer sewing machine, only this time creating a replica of a drum majorette's uniform. Lynn studied the picture from the McCalls pattern while her mother painstakingly stitched the white satin. The bodice was edged in gold braiding and brass buttons. The costume took shape after several fittings. The young director thought it was more beautiful than she could ever have imagined!

The day of the concert arrived. All the students wore black pants and white shirts. Hats made from construction paper were designed to fit each child's head size. In the chaos of outfitting every child, inevitably a mixup occurred and several students donned caps that were either too small or that hung over their eyes. Teacher constructed a tall drum major's headpiece with a gold tassel for Lynn. The morning rehearsal was flawless. They were ready.

That evening, the school parking lot filled quickly with parents' cars. All students were to arrive by six thirty. Then at seven sharp, the seventy students from both the morning and afternoon kindergarten classes marched onto the Washington School stage and took their positions. The dark velvet curtain slowly opened to reveal a packed house. Lynn spotted her parents in the front row.

Mildred sat tall in the green steel folding chair next to her husband. She quietly admired her handiwork. The sequence uniform that she'd sewn shimmered in the bright stage lights.

Mrs. Gustafson thrust the baton into Lynn's hand and pointed her toward the conductor's platform at the front of the stage. Slowly, the little director walked to the podium, stepped up, and faced her peers. Some classmates wondered why *she* had been chosen to be their director, except maybe her cousins. They already knew that Lynn was a show-off.

The audience was to her back, and all her classmates' eyes were attentive to the baton held high in her hand. Lynn was in control, and she knew it. She never forgot that moment on stage, nor did her classmates. She had been singled out, chosen once again to be in the limelight.

From that point on, Lynn became a leader. She exhibited a confidence as one moment became an hour and then rippled into days and years. During third grade, she bragged about becoming the youngest auntie in her class and of babysitting her nephew Todd Thomas. By fourth grade, she was sitting in the newly built Winterquist School only to have one desk conspicuously empty. Classmate Larry was crushed by a massive boulder on a rock pile at Meadowbrook Dairy.

Fifth grade was a cakewalk. Lynn believed she and her cousin were "teacher's pets." They decked out the class bulletins boards for every season and holiday while the rest of the class studied. The two girls brainstormed by putting their heads together and came up with some very unique and elaborate decorations. Once a project was completed, Lynn sat back at her desk and gazed at the end results with admiration. Mrs. Nynas knew exactly how to motivate, and this teacher's praise elevated Lynn's self-assurance.

During her fifth-grade year, dancing and acrobat lessons also birthed new creativity in Lynn. As a child, her mother never had these opportunities; so she made sure Lynn was exposed to tap, ballet, and tumbling.

Lynn attended Mary Lee's Dance Studio every Wednesday night. Her favorite part of the lesson was tumbling. A spring recital showcased what the students learned. Lynn, sparkling in a teal blue sequin leotard, performed an acrobatic solo with many flips, splits, walkovers, and cartwheels. Weeks later, the elementary school hosted a talent show. Lynn won first prize in her age group.

Before the end of the school year, cousin Warren and Lynn were featured artists at the Music Boosters meeting and performed a piano duet. The two were nearing the end of the piece when Lynn forgot a few notes and abruptly stopped. She threw her arms in the air and gasped! Warren was dumbfounded yet started laughing and so did the audience. Then Lynn joined in. The two abruptly stood, bowed, and walked back to their seats. The applause was as addictive as texting to a teen. Both Mrs. Sarkela, their piano teacher, and her son Dick, the high school band director, gave raving reviews to these young musicians. Life couldn't have been any better for the ten-year-old. Then along came sixth grade and the redheaded Wolfe.

Mrs. Wolfe was strict and demanded discipline. She noted Lynn's negative attitude toward academia and made her accountable. This teacher challenged lazy Lynn who attempted to take shortcuts. The red-haired spitfire had the nerve to discuss Lynn's casual attitude toward her studies with Mildred at an Esko Garden Society meeting. Both women were charter members and attended monthly meetings.

The mother confronted her daughter with the truth. As usual, Lynn made excuses for her bad behavior and then cried a bit to her mom when truth be told. But the next morning, she overheard her mother discuss the problem with her father.

Knowing Lynn was within earshot, Mildred spoke loudly, "Ray, I talked to Mrs. Wolfe at Garden Club last night. She told me that Lynn is not working up to her potential, and she has a bad attitude toward her studies."

Usually, Ray left disciplining and handling school issues to his wife. Yet Lynn knew she had disappointed her father. Never did she want to disappoint him. Very soon after the parent-teacher conversation, Lynn turned the corner and began to show serious progress in the classroom.

Beginning the last quarter of sixth grade, Mrs. Wolfe rewarded Lynn by appointing her as coeditor of the Winterquist elementary yearbook. The teacher saw leadership and organizational skills in the preteen. This appointment re-affirmed the girl's confidence, and she entered junior high on a positive note.

CHAPTER 25

A Stroke of Luck

Therefore, let us draw near with confidence to the
throne of GRACE, so that we may receive mercy and
find GRACE to help us in our time of need.
—Hebrews 4:16 (NASB)

THE HOSPITAL INTENSIVE UNIT WAS *quiet except for the occasional beep
from the monitor. Russ sat by his wife, wondering how to pray. He mused,*
Lynn would never want to be a vegetable and live all hooked up to
machines. If this stroke is irreversible, how can I tell my daughters
this news? Please, God, help us."

*Just then Chaplain Joan walked into the unit. She asked Russ,
"What is happening here? Why did Lynn return to the unit?"*

*Russ explained, "There's a possibility that Lynn had an ischemic
stroke."*

Together, they stepped back to the waiting room to tell the girls.

*Russ's eyes looked down at the floor as he calmly stated, "Ahhh, girls,
your mom isn't doing very well. The doctor thinks she had an irreversible
stroke." He couldn't bear to look at their fear-filled faces as he continued,
"They're watching her closely, and we need to pray."*

*With that cue, Chaplain Joan began a heartfelt prayer for Lynn
to come back to them that her recognition would return. She included
prayers for the family, as well.*

Yet their spirits and hope dipped to a new low. It was a crushing blow, and they could not understand. Word of this setback spread quickly throughout the little community of Esko and the surrounding area.

Prayer lines buzzed, and intercessors called for a miracle.

Russ watched as Lynn was wheeled off to radiology. The attending nurse walked into the unit.

She explained, "The nephrologist ordered another CAT Scan."

"What is a nephrologist?"

"A doctor specializing in kidney function, the care and treatment of kidney disorders," she explained.

"Oh," he paused, "I am so confused. First the doctors tell me Lynn's had a stroke. Then they tell me it might be irreversible!"

Thirty minutes passed, which seemed like thirty years to Russ. Finally, the patient returned from radiology. She was staring blankly at the ceiling.

"God, help her!" pleaded the distraught husband.

No sooner than he spoke, Dr. Yung, the kidney specialist, entered the ICU, with another colleague. He scanned Lynn's chart and the two doctors walked over to the window. They gazed upon the sparkling waters of Lake Superior while devising a plan of treatment.

Now Russ was angry and growing impatient. He pleaded with the nurse, "Why is that doctor just looking out the window?"

"He's thinking," she whispered.

Russ was silenced.

CHAPTER 26

Wedding Bell Blues

A man shall leave his father and mother and be united
to his wife, and the two will become one flesh.
—Matthew 19:5 (NIV)

SISTER JANET ASKED LYNN TO be a junior bridesmaid in her wedding. Well, she almost *had* to since she was her only sister. Of course, the preteen girl was thrilled.

Their older brother Rod married four years earlier.

"Why, Mom, can't I be the flower girl in Rodney's wedding? After all, I'm his sister," Lynn questioned her mother, who was attempting to console the little girl.

"I don't know. I guess they think you're too old."

Millie and Ray were concerned that their son was too young to marry. Rodney graduated from high school in May. The eighteen-year-old athlete had a bright future ahead of him...college, a basketball scholarship. But that was not to be. Lynn's brother was going to be a dad. He loved his girlfriend and would take responsibility for his actions.

The mother cried as she neatly packed her son's clothes into boxes. She knelt by his closet door in tears.

Meanwhile, Lynn cried because she couldn't be his flower girl. Just a year earlier, when she was in Marlene's wedding, she strolled down the same church aisle, tossing red rose petals.

So what had changed now that Big Brother was getting married? The answer was quite clear. The bride did not want the groom's immediate family involved. This treatment would continue indefinitely.

Three months after the wedding, the young wife gave birth to a premature son. He weighed less than five pounds, which required him to be monitored in an incubator for several days.

Yet there was much joy in the family when this baby boy entered the world. Four generations of Juntunens were living on the land Joseph acquired over eighty years earlier. Pictures were taken at the baptism, and Todd Thomas became the apple of his grandpa Ray's one eye.

Three and a half years later another son, Wade, arrived with a sweet smile and a sparkle in his eyes. Before he went to pre-school, he swam laps around the Midway swimming hole and donned a suntan darker than actor George Hamilton.

To provide for his family, Lynn's brother enrolled in barber school in Minneapolis where he stayed with Aunt Verna and her husband Reino. After completing courses and an internship in Duluth, he opened the Esko Barber Shop, affixed to his new home along Highway 61. Charlie Mannila's small convenience store once stood at the same site. Standing in its place was a charming two-story dwelling with an attached garage alongside the barber shop. Men and boys came to Rod's and discussed sports, the weather, local politics, and sometimes farming, while getting a quality haircut.

Years passed, and there was no quality time spent with his mother or sisters. Rod's marriage took precedence over a relationship with these women. Frustrated by this rejection, Lynn said things she later regretted.

"You ruined my brother!" the teen shouted out to her sister-in-law, all within earshot of a young nephew.

Those words were embedded into the child's memory and the woman's mind. Unfortunately, she would bring them up decades later.

Rod's parents and sisters counseled separately with the church pastor and even attended a forgiveness seminar. Still, nothing changed and any interaction was strained. Attempts to reconcile failed. Mistakes were made along the way.

After reading several books to gain a better understanding, Lynn realized she could not fix this relationship. Joyce Landorf Heatherly's book, *Irregular People*, was particularly helpful. No amount of forgiveness, love, or kindness would change the way her brother's wife viewed her or her mother. She experienced a cathartic revelation. Yet, she never gave up hope.

Lynn pleaded, "We're family, Let's try to get along."

The woman responded coldly, "You are not my family."

Often Mildred would cry and say, "I lost my son!" Everyone tried to console her; she was heart broken.

Fortunately, Ray was able to see Rod when he stopped by the barber shop for a haircut.

One day when the two were alone, the father warily asked his son, "Can Ma come to see you the next time I get my haircut?"

Sadly apologetic, Rod replied, "No, it's best if you leave well enough alone."

And so they did. Mildred stayed away and her prophetic statement uttered years earlier was fullfilled.

For forty years hair fell to the floor at the barber shop and was swept up with laughter and manly camaraderie. When Rod retired, customers missed the shop's social scene nearby Esko's Corner. Much like his father and grandfather, he provided a service to the small community and beyond. Not only successful as a local businessman, the barber, together with hs wife, successfully reared two sons, who became productive members of society.

Rejection by Rodney's wife was a painful pill to swallow that began when the little girl was eight years old and lasted a lifetime. Living with "what should have been" was never forgotten and only by God's grace was forgiveness possible, even if one wasn't forgiven.

Lynn purposefully and mindfully was thankful that she could resonate with others who were hurting and she could be a listening ear. Her family dilemma was not unique. Unfortunately, she discovered that many others experienced similar challenges within their family unit. They, too, needed to develop coping strategies, and learn how to deal with the negative emotions of frustration, anger, and bitterness.

So she never forgot because she was a better person for knowing the woman who married an only son, her only brother.

Most often two sisters are closer than a sister with a brother. That's why when Janet planned her wedding, she included her little sister in the wedding party. After high school the bride-to-be completed training in Duluth to become a licensed practical nurse. She moved back home to Esko and was employed by the Puumala Clinic, a family practice clinic in Cloquet. When springtime arrived, the bride began shopping for her September wedding dress. Since Duluth had four bridal stores, the bride visited them all.

Janet tried on several traditional gowns before she found the perfect one at Maurices Bridal Shoppe. To complete the ensemble, the bridal consultant waltzed from the curtained back of the shop carrying a delicate shoulder-length veil topped with a crown of pearls. Janet glowed as she twirled in front of the three-way mirror. Lynn's eyes welled with tears but then she quickly regained her composure. The young sister determined in her mind to be strong on the actual wedding day.

Seeing that Janet's wedding gown was chosen, the time came to select bridesmaid dresses. The bride wanted the dresses to complement the autumn-themed wedding. The junior bridesmaid watched in awe as cousin Susie tried on several tea-length gowns before a shimmery gold sheath dress with a satin back bow was approved of by all. The hemline was slightly below the knee and the quarter-length sleeves tapered before the elbow.

Because Lynn was so scrawny, the smallest dress size required considerable alterations. The bridal consultant called up the alterations lady from her sewing machine in the windowless back room of the store. A short lady with glasses hanging from a chain around her neck came running into the room. A bracelet of common pins wrapped around her left wrist. The seamstress knelt and stuck the dress with pins along the sides and hem. Lynn thought, *It will be a miracle if the lady gets that dress to fit me.*

The '60s fashion trend accessorized a formal dress with dyed-to-match heels. Maurice's Bridal Shoppe sold fabric shoes as well. The pumps were tinted to perfectly match the dress color. So, in one swift move of pen to checkbook, the mother of the bride paid for Janet's wedding gown, three matching bridesmaid dresses, and four pair of high-heeled shoes.

Final fittings occurred one week before the actual ceremony. Janet hoped to lose a few more pounds before the wedding, and Lynn hoped to gain a few.

When the big day arrived on September 19, the bride had everything in place. She chose this day because it was the same day her parents married twenty-four years earlier. Janet couldn't wait to become Mrs. Daniel Fredrick Pantsar, finally marrying her junior high school sweetheart.

On that brisk autumn eve, the pews in the church filled with over two hundred guests. Ushers seated everyone methodically while the wedding party fidgeted in the bridal room ready to make their entrance.

All of a sudden, there was a hush as the ushers carefully rolled the soft white runner down the aisle, taking great pains to keep it straight. Everyone recognized this as the sign that the ceremony was about to begin.

Lynn was the first to slowly wobble up the aisle to the front of the church. She was unaccustomed to walking in princess heels. One after the other, the bridesmaids followed. Finally, the bride came into view on the arm of her father. Overcome with emotion, Lynn watched while her only sister and her dear dad slowly kept step to Wagner's "Bridal Chorus." Janet was ready to meet her smiling groom, who waited at the altar.

No matter how hard Lynn tried, her tears would not stop. Quite embarrassed, the little junior bridesmaid also had difficulty standing in those dyed-to-match heels. Her skinny legs shook, and snot dripped from her nose. She was a mess and didn't even have a handkerchief.

After the ceremony concluded, the bridal party stood in a receiving line in the back of the church. Lynn stood there and sobbed while women hugged her and men squirmed uncomfortably.

"Oh, Lynn, it's going to be all right," Aunt Dottie consoled, yet the little girl with the crooked bangs only cried harder.

It wasn't as if she didn't like Danny. She did and wasn't losing a sister, but gaining a brother. Still Lynn knew life would be different because Janet would no longer live in the same house as her.

The wedding marked the beginning of the threesome: Mom, Dad, and Lynn. Janet moved only a mile and a half from her family's home into a sunny upstairs apartment with her husband. That's the way it was supposed to be. Janet waited until marriage to finally live with the man she loved. She fell for Dan way back in junior high but chose to follow the traditional path. Jan wanted to honor God, the institution of marriage, and her parents.

Yet before long, many couples would first live together before getting legally married. The sexual revolution was gearing up. It was the sixties, and the birth control pill was introduced. Free love and women's rights were generating as much controversy as the Vietnam War.

Back in Esko, the times weren't a-chang'n as quickly. The rural community was not as aware to the cultural changes occurring in the larger cities of the United States. Most certainly, the media was showing bits and pieces, but Lynn's world was still quite small. Free love was never really free. There were consequences to premarital sex, and Lynn would remember her mother's warning, "Why buy the cow when the milk's free?"

Come gather 'round people wherever you roam and admit that the waters around you have grown and accept it that soon you'll be drenched to the bone. If your time to you is worth savin', then you better start swimmin' or you'll sink like a stone, for the times they are a-changin'.

The line it is drawn, the curse it is cast. The slow one now, will later be fast. As the present now, will later be past. The order is rapidly fadin'. And the first one now, will later be last for the times they are a-changin'.

— *The Times They Are A Changin', Bob Dylan*

CHAPTER 27

Wonder Woman

Then the Lord God said, "It is not good for man to be
alone; I will make him a helper suitable for him."
—Genesis 2:18 (NASB)

JANET'S CANDLELIGHT WEDDING CEREMONY WAS steeped in traditional songs and meaningful scripture. Every attention to detail was made. To save money, the mother of the bride prepared most of the food for the reception, plus baking delicate petit fours. Likewise, as a keepsake, thank you gift, the bride cut costs by sewing sheer lace aprons for all who helped with the food and beverage service at the reception.

These tasks were accomplished all the while Mildred was enrolled in a pilot occupational therapy program in Duluth. It was the first one of its kind in the area. Mildred was like "Wonder Woman." At age forty-four, she surprised everyone when she decided to begin post-secondary classes and pursue another career.

This woman was a wonderful mother and devoted wife. Yet she envisioned herself helping others outside of the home. She didn't have a midlife crisis but a midlife epiphany.

Years earlier, John and Fannie Sunnarborg never encouraged Mildred to further her education after high school. No extra money was available to send a daughter to the teacher's college or nurse's training. Instead, Mildred was told by her father to get a job as a housekeeper or nanny with a wealthy Duluth family. Sadly, after graduation, she hopped the bus from Esko's Corner to Duluth and found employment with a prominent family.

For eighteen months, Millie, the maid, worked tirelessly as a servant for only a pittance. She learned quickly how the rich lived and saw opulence like never before. The lady of the manor was demanding, and the children were spoiled. After all the work was done for the day and the children sleeping in their rooms, Millie stepped slowly down the narrow servant's staircase into a small stark room behind the kitchen. It was cold and lonely, and she was homesick and in love.

This was not the life she hoped to have. The young woman missed the chaos of the Sunnarborg home, her parents, siblings, and boyfriend. Was she trapped, she wondered, living a life of servitude to an ungrateful, demanding mogul?

"No, sir!" she said out loud to herself.

And while sitting on the narrow bed in the dimly lit room, she devised a plan. The next day was Saturday, and her brother Clarence came with the car to take his sister back to Esko for the weekend.

Ray could hardly wait until the afternoon milking was finished. He took very little steam in the sauna and hurriedly washed up and dressed. Ray borrowed his dad's car and steered it toward the Sunnarborg farm where he knew "his girl" would be waiting. She bounded out the door happy to see her guy. They had been dating for two years.

"Do you want to come see Pa and Ma?" she asked.

"Sure, but we'll have to hurry and get to the show house by seven. My sister Bernice said this new movie *Gone with the Wind* is longer than two hours."

The couple visited with John and Fannie for a few minutes and then drove to the movie theater in Cloquet. Vivienne Leigh and Clark Gable starred in the epic film, and tears came to Millie's eyes several times during the motion picture. Once the theater lights came up, the couple exited into the spring night air, and Ray realized he was starving.

Since his father had given him extra money for this date, the two stopped by the Tulip Shoppe for hamburgers with fried onions and two fountain drinks. The check came to seventy-five cents, and after Ray paid the cashier, the two rode in silence back to Esko.

Ray parked the car in the Sunnarborg's driveway and commented, "You sure are quiet, Mildred. Are you feeling all right?"

Mildred swallowed hard trying her best to work up a little courage. Her boyfriend was about to receive an ultimatum.

Slowly, she began to speak, "The only time you and I are alone is in this car. If we are at each other's houses, our brothers and sisters fight for attention. I love you, and I think you love me. Right?"

Ray nodded, and she continued, "I'm not going to spend another winter shivering in your father's car since this is the only place we're alone. I think we should get married. What do you think, Ray?"

"Ya, sure," he quickly responded. "I'll come in and ask your Pa right now."

Mildred leaned over and hugged her man. Then, together, they walked up the porch steps hand in hand into the Sunnarborg farmhouse.

Mildred gave her two weeks' notice and left the life of a domestic and nanny. She returned to the quaint Finnish township and to the love of her life, Raymond Donald.

The two married on Thursday, September 19, 1940, amidst a sunny autumn afternoon. The wedding ceremony took place at the church's parsonage with only the parents, Grandpa Joseph, and the attendants present. Mildred's sister Gladys was the matron of honor, and Allen, Ray's brother, fulfilled the duties of the best man. Reverend Nelson officiated speaking in English even though Joseph wanted the vows spoken in Finnish.

The mother of the bride, Fannie insisted, "This is the USA, and in this country, people speak English."

Mildred wore a deep blue two-piece suit with no hat or veil. Ed bought the groom a double-breasted suit with matching tie for the occasion, since Ray had outgrown his confirmation "*Riipikolla*" suit.

The father of the bride, John Sunnarborg, paid for the food at the reception which was held the following Sunday afternoon at the Ed and Esther Juntunen home. Miniature ice cream cups were a special addition to the wedding cake and a favorite among the children. There was no dance, no liquor…just a simple wedding where vows were spoken and honored.

Twenty-four years after the wedding, Millie was sensing a change. The Women's Liberation Movement was just beginning, and this woman was ahead of her time. Her brave, adventurous spirit proved that goals could be achieved whenever a person was ambitious and dared to revamp the course of their life.

Her mind was made up. Mildred was going back to school. She researched several options and decided to explore the medical field. The first-ever program offered in Duluth fulfilled all the requirements to earn a degree as an occupational therapy assistant (OTA).

With her husband's support and approval, she became a student once again. Monday through Friday, rain or shine, for twelve months, she drove twenty miles to classes at the Barnes Ames building in Duluth.

To the amazement of her family, Millie earned the degree all the while continuing the daily duties of caring for her household and extended family. She fulfilled a year of internship at the Duluth hospital, St. Mary's, near the watchful eye of Sr. Eugenia Panger, a Benedictine nun. While under her tutelage, Mildred's bigotry and prejudice toward Catholicism slowly dissolved.

After completing the internship, she was hired in Cloquet at the newly built Convalescent Care Nursing Home adjacent to the hospital. Mildred was given free reign to create the nursing home's first occupational therapy department. She ordered state-of-the-art equipment and supplies. Like a child waiting for Christmas morning to arrive, Millie waited anxiously for the many packages and boxes to appear by her office door.

The new department, modeled similarly to the one where she interned, was located on the lower floor of the nursing home. Its expansive windows overlooked the picturesque St. Louis River and hillside of Norway pines. Residents engaged in crafts that included rug looming, pottery, and woodworking. The hands-on therapy was designed to improve dexterity, memory, and motor skills.

Many of the nursing home's occupants were of Finnish descent, and Mildred spoke *Suomi* with them. Being bilingual, she was a valuable asset to the staff especially when a frustrated resident could not communicate with a nurse or doctor. Often, Millie was summoned from the OT Department to interpret.

Three years later, Mildred's mother was placed in the nursing home. Aging Fannie could no longer live on the family farm. Because she was Mildred's mother, she was given extra special care. Fannie never participated in her daughter's occupational therapy program. Instead, she visited with her large family, who came by often, and between patients, Mildred spent time with her beloved mother.

After Fannie's death, she worked five more years at the hospital before taking an early retirement. The family accountant discovered that after income taxes were filed, working at the hospital was hardly profitable. Moreover, her baby Lynn was in high school and soon would leave the nest.

As quickly as Millie embarked on a second career, she wasted no time returning to, what she considered her most important job, taking care of Ray and Lynn Rae. The three quickly settled back into a routine. Father and daughter were thankful to have the lady of the house "in house" full- time. Besides, Millie was happy she didn't have to get to work before the crack of dawn and multitask two careers.

In retrospect, valuable lessons were learned by stepping out of her comfort zone, daring to become a student and later securing the position as head of a newly established department in the nursing home.

Millie challenged herself in midlife, as Lynn did too. Much like her mother, Lynn at forty changed careers and was being groomed for promotion until that fateful day in February, when everything changed.

Chapter 28

Pet Sounds

A righteous man cares for the needs of his animal.
> —Proverbs 12:10 (NIV)

THE BEACH BOYS IN 1966 released the very popular album Pet Sounds. Long before the singing group and their sensational record hit stores, the little girl with crooked bangs was listening keenly to barks and meows. First, was Sparky, the dog whose yelping and swimming around and around in the deep interrupted swimming at the river. A few years later uncle Willie's dog Sandy had a litter of ten puppies. Sparky was the father. One female puppy had similar markings to her dad Sparky but shorter fur like her mother, Sandy, a Golden Labrador.

Uncle Willie convinced Lynn that this pup should be hers. He planted the seed, Lynn's pleading tears watered it. In the end, Mildred and Ray suddenly had two dogs to feed. The little girl named the puppy Mittens because of her snow- white paws.

Ray carried home from the milk house a large cardboard box strewed with a layer of straw. That first night the scared puppy howled away in the basement. She missed her mommy. Lynn understood. In the same way, when she stayed overnight at somebody's house, she was scared, too. That's why the little girl left her warm bed and went into the cold basement where the puppy was crying out. Lynn comforted Mittens by petting her fur and scratching her little ears. Lynn curled up inside the large cardboard box and before long fell asleep with her new friend.

When Millie was ready for bed she went down to the basement and discovered her sleeping daughter. Mittens barely opened her eyes, then yawned as Millie placed a ticking clock next to the dog and carried the child back to her bedroom. Thankfully everyone slept through the night.

The next morning Lynn awoke and darted down to the basement only to discover the puppy not moving. She nudged the dog fearing it was dead. Mittens jumped up and began licking the little girl's fingers. Lynn squealed as she lifted the puppy from the box and kissed its cold nose. Without a minute to spare, the two made their way up the steps and outside where the dog watered the grass.

Mittens grew quickly and became a constant companion. She followed the little girl all around the neighborhood, except if a thunderstorm was brewing. At any distant crack of thunder, Mittens ran home and darted into the basement where her body trembled long after the storm subsided. The girl decided that Grandma Juntunen probably understood.

Before Mittens was spayed she had two litters of twelve and thirteen puppies. Lynn sat in the doghouse with them and later worried obsessively once new homes were found for them. She believed no one would love those puppies as much as she. Her parents disagreed, placed an ad in the newspaper FREE Lab/Border Collie Mix PUPPIES and all were adopted.

Once Sparky died, another pet made sounds in the house. A calico kitten from the barn joined the family and before long she was having kittens of her own. Her name was Big Ushi (a very strange, made-up name) and she meowed for thirteen years.

Lynn talked to her in a high-pitched voice which was exclusively "cat talk." Mostly she was a house cat, but once outside her hunting instincts kicked in. The feline brought back countlesss mice and birds that she proudly dropped onto the back patio for Lynn to admire. For added attention Big Ushi flipped them into the air and playfully pawed them. After the hunting escapades, she meowed loudly by the door signaling for anyone to let her in. Once in the house she found a warm spot by the heat vent in the living room and meticulously groomed herself by licking her fur for several minutes and purring continuously. After her bath she curled up in a circle and took a long nap.

When the Christmas season arrived, Millie bought a fresh Norway pine. Before Ray came home for lunch, she dragged the tree to an inside corner of the living room and plopped it into a small red stand. Red and blue lights and shiny balls were added to the soft green limbs. Then Millie sat in her rocker for a moment gazing at the tree with admiration, but only for a moment.

That evening after supper the family went visiting to Lola and Ernie's. Lynn always liked going there to play with her cousins Darrell and Keith. When they returned home, the Christmas tree was toppled over. Fragments from the ornaments were scattered on the thick carpeting, but the white angel tree topper remained intact.

"That darn cat must've tried to climb our tree!" Mom told anyone in hearing distance.

Raymond helped his wife reposition the tree back to its rightful place. During the night while asleep, they heard a loud crash in the living room.

"That darn *kissa* (cat) tipped over our tree again!", Millie alleged.

The next morning, she got out her trusty hammer and three sixteen penny nails from the tool drawer. Then she fiercely pounded them through the holes in the tree stand, through the gray wool carpeting, and straight into the hardwood floor!

"Bang, bang, bang" pounded the hammer.

"I'll fix that cat!" she mumbled under her breath.

Thereafter, every Christmas tree that graced the living room during the holidays remained upright and beautiful, thanks to sixteen penny nails.

Big Ushi was more independent than the dogs until she was going to deliver kittens. Beforehand Lynn place a cardboard box with a doll blanket on a chair in the basement. That was designated as the" labor room." The little girl watched and waited for signs that her cat was in labor. Before long, the *kissa's* pleading eyes met Lynn's accompanied by a long, drawn out meow. It was time.

Big Ushi meowed and meowed until Lynn sat beside the prepared box. While nurse Lynn stroked the cat's tummy crooning gently, the swollen belly tightened and contracted until the kittens were born. If Lynn left the "labor room," the cat followed her even if a kitten was ready to pop out. Thus, Lynn became midwife to her cat, who delivered a litter three times annually.

Regretfully looking back, Big Ushi should've been spayed. Yet only once was she taken to the Cloquet Veterinarian Clinic, when she was euthanized for bladder cancer by the same vet who made house calls to Meadowbrook's cows. Dr. Pattison comforted Lynn, who sobbed as she explained to the kind doctor that for the past thirteen years she grew up alongside that cat with the strange name, Big Ushi. The seasoned veterinarian exhibited compassion and no doubt comforted many a pet owner.

The beloved companions were laid to rest under the tall elm by the edge of the river when pet sounds were silenced.

CHAPTER 29

Coming of Age

We must turn all of our educational efforts to training our
children for the choices which will confront them. The child,
who is to choose wisely, must be healthy in mind and body.
—Coming of Age in Samoa, Margaret Mead

MARGARET MEAD WROTE *THE COMING of Age in Samoa* in 1928. As
a young anthropologist, she studied the maturation process of the
Samoan tribe. Lynn read the book for an English report about the
time she was "coming of age." Written over thirty years prior, Mead's
words were pertinent to a time in Lynn's life when the sexual revolution and women's rights were being hotly debated.

Mead lived among the Samoans, and from her observations,
various conclusions were drawn concerning the attitudes of girls
toward their families, their religious interest or lack of it, and details
of their sex lives. Lynn was curious about these women living in a
very different culture. She was curious because at the time, she was
in her formative adolescent years.

Entering junior high in September of 1964 marked excitement
as well as humility. The wedding and seventh grade dominated Lynn's
thoughts. She felt so grown up being in her sister's wedding, even
though she was ten days shy of being only twelve years old. On the
contrary, she was nervous and unsure of the new school surroundings, friendships, and her ever-changing body.

Although Mead's book fascinated this young adolescent girl, parts of the content upset many Westerners when first published in 1928. At that time, many American readers felt shocked by Mead's observation that young Samoan women deferred marriage for many years while enjoying casual sex. They eventually married, settled down, and successfully reared their own children.

Was this a foreshadowing to what would happen to girls in the sixties and beyond?

After Janet's wedding, everyone went back to business and school. For the little girl with crooked bangs, seventh grade proved to be quite different from elementary school.

The start of school meant "school clothes shopping." Entering junior high was a huge milestone, so a girl's wardrobe needed extra special attention. The fall Sears and J. C. Penney catalogs arrived in July. Lynn spent hours stretched out on the living room floor, paging through the thick colorful books. Dresses, skirts, sweaters, coats, and shoes shouted out from those shiny pages: "Buy me! Buy me!"

Lynn couldn't decide what to order. Most of the teen-size clothes were too large for her petite frame. Her persistent search paid off and she found a few items. By early August, the order form was carefully filled out, making sure all the item letters, numbers, and sizes were correct. Then Mom made a final check and asked a few questions. Next Lynn "called in" the order by phone to the local office, making certain every item number and letter were correct. No credit cards existed to confirm payment. Instead the kind voice on the other end took all the necessary information and concluded the conversation with a delivery date. The catalog order was either mailed directly to the house for a small fee or shipped to the Cloquet location at no additional cost. Consequently, most of the time when the order arrived, it was picked up at the catalog office on the next trip to "town."

Back to school shopping also entailed at least one trip to downtown Duluth to the big department stores. During the early fifties, no malls existed in the Unites States. Shopping was done primarily by strolling outdoors from store to store. All that began to change when the very first mall named Southdale opened its doors in 1956 near Edina, Minnesota. The concept of a fully enclosed, climate-controlled building housing many stores became so popular that today there is at least one mall in every city in the nation.

Lynn never heard from her parents the words we can't afford this. She assumed that within reason she could get what she wanted. Lynn never demanded; she asked. When she was told, "No, maybe another time," Lynn listened, knowing very well that her mother appreciated fine clothes too. They'd return to the department store another day.

Once again, without realizing it, Lynn was getting lessons in economics. She watched and learned the value of money and its power. Her middle-class parents worked hard and budgeted every paycheck. This allowed Lynn the luxury of wearing new shoes and stylish clothes. Many would agree that Lynn Rae was spoiled. The girl did not understand anything different.

By junior high, both her brother and sister were married. She was the baby, the lone bird left in the nest, and quite frankly, she enjoyed being an "only child." She had her mom and dad all to herself for eight years before she flew the coop.

Mead in her book concluded that Samoan girls belonged to a stable monocultural society, surrounded by role models, and where nothing concerning the basic human facts of copulation, birth, bodily functions, or death was hidden. By comparison, the Samoan girl was not pressured to choose from among a variety of conflicting values, as was the American girl.

The passage from childhood to adulthood in Samoa was a smooth transition, not marked with emotional distress, anxiety, or confusion unlike the girls' coming of age in the United States.

Junior high girls were much the same everywhere in the States. The girl with crooked bangs was traumatized while she was miserably trying to become a woman. She wanted to fit in to the status quo yet wanted to be noticed.

The first junior high choir concert was very humbling. Since the school did not have choir robes for junior high students, the director asked that girls wear white blouses and black skirts. The boys were required to wear white shirts and black pants. Black shoes completed the ensemble.

Since Lynn already had princess heels, a low pump with a tiny heel, from Janet's wedding. She decided that they'd be perfect for the concert, once they were dyed black.

The night of the performance arrived, and she confidently paraded into the choir room. Much to Lynn's chagrin, some girls made fun of her low-heeled shoes.

One girl was particularly cruel and sneered, "Oh, see what Lynn Juntunen has on. She thinks she's so hot!"

Lynn's eyes looked down while her princess heels clicked along the tiled floor as she passed by the heckler.

During the concert, her stomach ached, and she felt like fainting on the risers. The evening seemed to never end for Lynn, who wanted to get away from the taunting girls. Having performed first, the seventh-grade students went back to a classroom to wait for the junior and senior choirs to finish their vocals.

Finally, the last song was sung, and the audience was dismissed. Lynn rushed out of the choir room, looking for her mom among the people shuffling through the hallway.

Later at home in the privacy of her bedroom, she quietly cried into her pillow and thought, *Sticks and stones will break my bones, but names will never hurt me.* But they did. Lynn never again wore the princess heels to a school function, and she never forgot how cruel words spoken by a "friend" crushed her heart.

Sadly, Lynn did not learn from the experience. Later, she forgot and spewed hurtful words to others, as well. Perhaps it was a rite of passage for teens to cut down each other. In her insecurity, Lynn attempted to build herself up by thoughtless remarks and cruel gossip. Ultimately, the spoken word became like a two-edged sword, cutting both ways.

Times for the girl whose bangs were no longer crooked were bewildering.

"It was the best of times, it was the worst of times, it was the age of wisdom, it was the age of foolishness, it was the epoch of belief, it was the epoch of incredulity, it was the season of Light, it was the season of Darkness, it was the spring of hope, it was the winter of despair." (Charles Dickens from The Tale of Two Cities).

CHAPTER 30

Roses for Recovery

The desert shall bloom like the rose.
—Isaiah 35:1 (KJV)

DR. YUNG NEVER GREW TIRED *of the view from the windows facing the Duluth harbor. The glistening, clear water calmed him and gave him clarity when faced with medical decisions. Slowly he shifted his eyes back to the inside of the room and to the husband sitting by his wife's bedside.*

Then he spoke very slowly, "Mr. Davidson, as we once thought, we don't believe your wife had a DVT (deep-vein thrombosis), a clot that breaks loose from her broken femur, causing a stroke. It appears that she has a sodium deficiency. Her sodium levels are dangerously low. We're not quite sure why but, we will begin an IV drip. It is critical that we slowly introduce sodium back into Lynn's body, since it is an essential electrolyte to regulate blood pressure and is needed for proper muscle and nerve cell functioning. We will get this right and will keep a close eye on the patient."

Hearing those words, Russ became inwardly incensed. What was he to believe? Who was he to believe? His brain was not digesting this additional information. All he knew was that his wife appeared to be in a vegetative state just staring into space.

Surgery to rod Lynn's femur was postponed because of the sodium deficiency. As her body recovered from the shock, Russ allowed no visitors into the ICU, not even his daughters. All alone, he sat by Lynn's bedside, confused and frightened. He refused to believe the doctors or nurses when they told him she would regain consciousness. Too much had happened in the course of the last seven days. Lynn opened her eyes and, without expression, stared at her husband. He prayed and bargained with God. "Please bring Lynn back to me," he mumbled.

A male nurse working the afternoon shift looked in on his patient. Outside the unit on a metal cart sat a vase filled with a dozen long-stemmed yellow roses. Live flower arrangements or plants were not allowed in the private cubicle. However, this nurse took exception. From the vase, he pulled one stem with a huge blossom and carried it over to the hospital bed.

As he gently placed it upon Lynn's chest, he spoke, "See how beautiful is this rose? Can you smell it?"

The yellow petals touched her nose, and her nostrils wiggled. It appeared as if Lynn understood the nurse and smelled the fragrant rose.

Russ gasped and hoped. Is this another sign? Could his beloved be coming out from this stupor?

CHAPTER 31

Relationships

Two are better than one. If one falls down,
her friend can help her up.
—Ecclesiastes 4: 9,10 (NIV)

ENTERING EIGHTH GRADE WAS SLIGHTLY comforting. No longer rookies at school, Lynn and her classmates were familiar with the building, opening lockers, and social groupings. Cliques were developing and soon students unknowingly fell into positions with the jocks, or hoods, the smart "nerdy" kids, or the "in" crowd. In September, Lynn became a teenager and a B-team cheerleader, along with her best friend, Sheri. The two did everything together. Music, clothes, boys, and junior high dances defined their lives. Their group included cousins Sandy and Karen, who were a year older, and Vicki, another B-squad cheerleader. Since at that time, girls could not participate in competitive sports; getting on the cheerleading squad was the next best thing. The six positions on the B squad and six on the A squad were highly sought after by girls in grades 8–12.

Practice sessions for games were held after school. The girls rehearsed their cheers and stunts in the hallway while the boys passed the ball and ran plays in the adjacent Lincoln gym. Lynn and Sheri patiently waited for the boys' basketball team to end their practice. They stood by the lockers until two particular boys appeared. Freshly showered and exhausted from the strenuous workout, the tired basketball players stopped to chat, exchanging only a few short sentences. But that's all the girls needed. They were happy with the brief conversation. Sheri had a crush on Gerry and Lynn had an interest in Russ. Hmmmmm? Where was this going? Unfortunately, these freshmen boys were more concerned about basketball than two eighth-grade girls.

During the following summer, a newly constructed arena/auditorium in Duluth opened. It became the venue for all major sporting events and concerts. Never before was there an opportunity to see popular rock and roll artists on tour. The young teenagers screamed for pop bands the Monkees, Herman's Hermits, the Beach Boys, and Paul Revere & the Raiders. How exciting to see these famous musicians performing live.

Both Sheri and Lynn were the youngest children in their families. Their fathers were Esko classmates and longtime friends. Their mothers belonged to a women's "sewing club" where more chatting was done than actual sewing. Nevertheless, Sheri and Lynn were stitched together tighter than the Meadowbrook bull's ass in fly season. Like typical junior high girls with similar interests, the two were connected at the hip. Rarely was one seen without the other.

Unfortunately, by the time they got to high school their interests changed and so had they. Lynn continued to advance to the A-squad in tenth grade and cheered for the boys' football and basketball teams for three years. Pep fests, decorating halls, practices, and games consumed her time.

Even though Sheri and Lynn moved on to new friendships, they never forgot the fun-filled junior high moments. Yet, the years marched along to senior high.

The first school social activity of the year was always a Sadie Hawkins dance, sponsored by the cheerleaders. As a sophomore and cheerleader, Lynn was involved with planning this "girl-ask-boy" function. Early on, Lynn knew that she wanted to invite a certain junior boy. Similarly two girls had the same idea.

In spite of that, Russ accepted Lynn's invitation, and thus began their courtship, which wasn't all moonlight and roses. There were ups and downs along the way, yet asking Russ to this dance was a clear signal that the girl with the crooked bangs was growing up and was very interested in the skinny junior boy with the crooked teeth in braces. Neither were experienced in dating. Certainly both of them liked others in elementary and junior high, nothing serious. But they were older now and in high school. The Sadie Hawkins dance was the beginning of a five-year courtship.

During the Friday afternoon football game, Esko defeated Carlton 35-13. Russ played the position of flanker and was back-up quarterback to Darrell, who threw for five touchdown passes that day. Since the field was not equipped with lights, the game was played at 3:00 p.m. on grass turf next to the Lincoln High School. When the horn sounded to end the game, the jubilant team barreled into the locker room, quickly showered, and dashed home for supper. The cheerleaders, including Lynn, stayed at the school in order to decorate the gym for the Hillbilly-themed dance.

Once the gym was transformed into Lil' Abner and Daisy Mae's barn dance, the girl made a beeline home to get ready. Lynn inhaled goulash with her parents and then excused herself to get ready for the dance. She took extra time to apply a light makeup and pearlized pink lipstick to match her pink mohair sweater. Her bangs were no longer crooked, since a beautician, not Mildred, cut her hair. She wore it short, trimmed above the ears, which was the latest style. Smiling at her reflection in the bathroom mirror she thought, *Hmmm, I wonder if Russ will dance with me tonight?*

Boys aren't very good dancers, she concluded, and time would tell. Then she bounced down the hallway toward the living room, where her parents were watching Chet Huntley and David Brinkley broadcasting the nightly news on TV. The Vietnam War was escalating, and cousin Terry Sunnarborg was overseas, fighting the Vietcong in the Mekong Delta. Every night, casualties were announced; yet to many Americans, including Lynn, the unpopular war seemed distant and surreal.

Being the typical myopic teen, her major concerns involved boys, cheerleading, and friendships. Current world events held very little interest to Lynn, unlike her mother, who was making arrangements to send a Christmas care package to nephew Terry in Vietnam.

Several dozen cookies, toothpaste, canned goods, soap, and candy were lovingly packed into a huge cardboard box which was shipped to Terry's barracks. Years later, Terry sadly admitted that he never received the care packages. No doubt they were intercepted by the enemy.

Interrupting the nightly news stories, Lynn announced to her parents, "Can somebody drop me off at the school now to sell tickets?"

"Sure, do you want me to pick you up after the dance then?" Millie inquired.

"Ya, if you could. The dance lasts until ten o'clock. I'll come out the side doors by the lunchroom, okay?"

"Ya, Dad or I will be there. Most likely it'll be me, since Dad has to get up for milking early in the morning."

Lynn hated to bother her parents to chauffeur her everywhere, but since she didn't have a driver's license, nor did any of her friends, the mom and dad Uber service would have to suffice for now.

The sun was setting in the west as mother and daughter got into the Ford Galaxy and drove to the Sadie Hawkins dance at the school. Mildred parked at the curb just long enough for Lynn to jump out. She thought, *My baby is growing up and attending school dances. I wonder if tonight she's hoping to dance with that Davidson boy.*

Oblivious to her mother's thoughts and absorbed in her own, Lynn hurried through the gym doors and never looked back.

A subtle change was occurring with the dynamics of mother and daughter. Lynn wanted independence, to think for herself. Her mother never stifled Lynn's need to break out and slowly become her own person. Millie drove back to the three-bedroom ranch house sensing it wouldn't be long before the last fledgling would leave the nest and fly away.

Girls began to arrive with their dates. As Lynn sold tickets at the front desk, she kept glancing toward the door. Finally, Russ and his friends Dennis and Gerry strolled in.

When he bent down to purchase a ticket, Lynn beamed shyly and said, "Oh, you don't have to pay, I've got it. Go on in, and I'll meet you in a little while. Right now, I have to sell tickets until seven thirty."

Russ, with his buddies not far behind, cruised into the Hillbilly-themed gymnasium and looked around. They spotted girls from their grade and walked over to the familiar faces. The band began to play, and because the music was so loud, conversations were impossible. Consequently, everyone stood along the edges of the dance floor, waiting for a cue. Yet nobody danced until a new girl from Proctor grabbed her date by his hand. She pulled him out onto the floor where they stood facing each other. Others followed suit, and the dance officially began. Two fast songs followed: "Twist and Shout" by the Beatles and "Let's Spend the Night Together" by the Rolling Stones.

Oh, boy, Russ thought with panic, *I don't know how to dance, and this is a dance!* Just then Lynn sauntered over and flashed him her best smile. He relaxed a bit as the band slowed down the tempo with the Beach Boys hit song, "In My Room." Couples straggled into the center of the gym where girls placed their arms around the guy's neck, and the two rocked from left foot to right foot…back and forth, back and forth to the slow rhythm of the song.

Lynn grasped Russ's hand and pulled him forward, saying, "Come on, let's dance." He was about to shake his head no when he realized she was walking out on the dance floor. What could he do? After all, she asked him to this dance, and he did like her. So he gingerly followed.

She turned to find him by her side. Reaching up for his neck, she curled her thin arms around his shoulders and swayed back and forth. Russ wanted to run but knew he was trapped for the moment. Lynn placed her head on his chest and breathed in the sweet scent of a freshly starched shirt. His heart was pounding as he worried this girl could smell the nervous sweat dripping down his back.

The song ended, and the two walked slowly back to the safety of the group. Others could talk, and they could listen, much easier to do than carrying on a one-on-one conversation while slow dancing. Lynn danced a few fast songs with her girlfriends. Before long the clock on the wall neared ten. Very shortly, her mom would be waiting at the curb.

So it was, the evening ended early for Lynn. Although hopeful, she wondered how long it might take for Russ to get up enough courage to ask her out?

All weekend, Lynn thought about the dance and Russell. She couldn't wait for Monday to return to school. The moment she walked into the building, a flock of girls surrounded her locker.

"Did you hear who Russ rode home with after the dance on Friday night?" Susie asked.

"No, who?"

"We saw Russ get into the car with another girl and Jenny," clucked Susie.

Fighting back tears, Lynn thought her chest was going to cave in. She quickly turned the paddle lock to its correct combination and jerked open her green locker. The sophomore locker lobby was near the washrooms. Not uttering another word, Lynn grabbed her first-hour English lit book and second-hour geometry textbook and slammed shut the locker door. Everyone in the hall stopped what they were doing and stared at Lynn as she darted into the washroom and into a stall. She needed privacy, enough time to regain her composure before facing another person.

Instead of walking by Russ's locker, the heartbroken teen took a different route to get to her first-hour class. Fortunately, after taking roll, Mrs. Pearson, the English teacher, assigned students to read the next three chapters, then added that there would be no discussion or quiz that morning. Unfortunately, to add insult to injury, the class was reading Shakespeare's *Romeo and Juliet*.

Lynn shifted uncomfortably in her seat and kept her head bent low into the book, but reread the first paragraph over and over again. She couldn't concentrate on Romeo and Juliet. That love story would have to wait. Lynn needed to plan her next move with her own "Romeo Russell."

Throughout the next week, Lynn talked to no one about the events after the dance. She avoided Russ until one day in the library she came face-to-face with him by the nonfiction bookcases.

"Hi." He smiled and continued, "I haven't seen you around."

"Oh, I've been pretty busy," Lynn coolly responded.

"Halloween's on Tuesday night. Do you want to come trick or treating with us? We might get a few eggs."

Lynn knew exactly what that meant. A few of his buddies were going to get rotten eggs from a local vendor, Otto's. Then they planned to run around Esko and throw eggs at cars and houses.

She hesitated, purposely appearing unenthusiastic, and remarked, "Maybe I'll run into you later."

Then she quickly walked past him to chat with a senior boy who was sitting at the next table, reading the sports section from the *Duluth Tribune*. She lingered there for only a minute, flirted with the young man, then exited the library.

I'll just make him jealous, Lynn decided. Everyone knew the senior star running back wanted to date her. But he had a reputation as being a fast mover, and frankly, Lynn was frightened to be alone with him. Russ needn't know that. All the girl wanted was to create the illusion that other guys were interested in her.

Halloween was the next day. After school, Lynn searched the attic for the box of Halloween costumes. She found two scary masks and the kitten costume she wore in fifth grade. Maybe she'd be a cowgirl, she thought, and wear jeans, boots, and a small black mask that covered only her eyes.

Lynn ate an early supper and prepared to go trick or treating once darkness fell. She met up with Vicki and cousin Karen and the three traipsed all over the Northridge neighborhood. When she reached the Esko stoplights, she eyed Russ leaning against the pole.

He hollered, "Hey, Lynn, come on with me and Den."

"Okay," she yelled back and, turning to Karen and Vicki, asked, "Do you want to come with us?"

"No way," together they chimed, and Karen added, "We're going back to Vicki's house."

And so they left Lynn with the boys and their two dozen eggs.

Suddenly, the town constable's car was sighted in the distance. The teens ran helter-skelter through the school yard crossing Highway 61. The boys were quickly outpacing Lynn, who was getting farther and farther behind. They were running lickety-split through people's yards.

All at once, Lynn slipped and fell on the dewy grass. Someone grabbed her arm and shouted, "Hey, where are you going?"

Lynn peered through the dark night to discover the person was none other than Russ's uncle Ervin.

"Ahhh, I don't know," the girl answered. Russ turned around and walked back over to where Lynn was standing.

"Ahhh, hi," Russ sheepishly greeted his uncle.

"Where are you running?" asked Ervin.

"I dunno, just bringing Lynn home," retorted the nephew as he fiddled with the three eggs remaining in his jacket pocket.

"Well, you better get moving then. It's getting late," Ervin warned as he turned away and smiled ever slightly.

About a week later, Russell asked Lynn on their first official date. It was with another couple—Lynn's cousin Craig and his date, Judy. Double dating was less stressful. Besides, Russ had very limited access to his parents' vehicle, while Craig drove his own car, a 1952 Chevy, which was dubbed "the green goose." The boys picked up Lynn and drove to Palkie Road where Judy lived with her widowed father. Ironically, these two couples dated young, married young, and remained friends for the rest of their lives.

Chapter 32

The Power of One

> I am only one, but I am one. I cannot do
> everything, but I can do something.
>
> —Edward Everett Hake

WHEN ONE PERSON INFLUENCES A few others, there are two major effects: a ripple effect that in time could impact thousands and a broadening effect since one person influences many.

Employers, teachers, family, friends. They all have an impact on our lives. As impressionable teenagers, when we are attempting to develop our value system, one person can change the complexion of an entire grade and beyond.

Lynn's sophomore year of high school was rather pivotal. One girl influenced several others. This new girl from Superior was a smart, brassy, and streetwise girl who arrived in hick town, USA. Jo missed her Wisconsin buddies and begged to move back to Superior. But that was not to be, and this angered the girl. Since her mother wanted Jo to make new friends, she encouraged her daughter to host parties. These gatherings were held with very little supervision, a perfect prescription for teenage trouble. Underage drinking and cigarette smoking were glamorized. Kids were validated if they got drunk.

This rebellious girl became very influential, a Pied Piper leading others down a slippery slope. Booze, smoking, cursing, and defiant behavior were part of belonging to this "in" crowd. Meanwhile, the "goody-goodys" followed the rules, were respectful, and excluded from the clique.

In the final analysis, Jo must not be totally blamed for the girls falling under her spell. Unrest fueled young people, who were living in the Age of Rebellion. After all, it was the sixties ushering in the sexual revolution, the "pill," the women's movement, and antiwar demonstrations.

One question remained: how could the power of one sustain so much clout? It was quite simple. Because several female leaders in the class relinquished their power, didn't want to rock the boat, went along with the crowd. The ripple effect of those choices lasted for years to follow.

As long as Lynn asked Russ to the Sadie Hawkins dance months earlier, she hoped he would reciprocate and invite her to the spring prom. Two weeks before the event, Russ finally did. Two days later, Lynn and her mother shopped for formals at an exclusive bridal boutique in Duluth. A mint green gown with white trim was selected with few alterations required. Delicate rhinestone earrings, white elbow length gloves, and a white fur cape completed the ensemble.

Several of Lynn's friends were dating upperclassmen. Between classes, the girls chattered endlessly about the gala, and finally, the day of prom arrived. Mildred's beautician fixed Lynn's hair with a wiglet of small curls on the crown. Lynn polished her fingernails light pink and carefully applied her makeup. Mother helped her daughter zipping and snapping the gown in the back. Janet drove over to take a few pictures with her new Instamatic camera. She left toddlers Keith and Tom at home with her husband.

When Russ, looking quite handsome in a white dinner jacket arrived with his dad's Chevy Biscayne, he seemed very nervous. His fingers shook as he handed the fragrant white orchid corsage to his date. He thought, *Why did I even ask Lynn to the prom?*

Then just as quickly as those thoughts floated into his mind, Russ was jolted back to reality as the girl exclaimed, "The flowers are so big and beautiful. Thank you!"

Janet handed her sister the white box containing the boutonniere. Lynn presented Russ with a mint green carnation that perfectly matched the color of her gown. She looked up, smiled at him, and carefully pinned it on his lapel. The camera flashed and caught the moment.

"There," she announced and playfully tapped his sleeve. "Let's take a few pictures in the living room, okay?"

Russ followed sheepishly and posed as best he could given the fact that he felt jittery and his hands were cold and clammy. After the photo op ended, Russ breathed a sigh of relief. "I never want to do that again."

From the kitchen window, Mildred and Janet peeked through the yellow cafe curtains, watching as the young man carefully opened the car door for his date and then drove away with Lynn.

Janet snickered to her mother. "Boy, Russell sure was nervous when we were taking pictures. Just what would he be like someday if he got married?"

The two laughed at the thought, not knowing this prophecy would be fulfilled in just about four years.

During math class the following Monday, the teacher Mr. Anderson, who was a prom chaperone, teased Russ about his dancing skills.

"Russ Davidson looked like a boa constrictor on the dance floor. He wrapped his arms so tightly around his prey, Lynn Juntunen."

It provided a little post-prom humor for the algebra class at the expense of Russell, who shrugged down in his desk with embarrassment.

Weeks later, the same teacher told Russ that Lynn was not a good influence and he shouldn't be dating her. There was some validity in the warning. Lynn was not a serious math student and did just enough to get by in Mr. Anderson's class. Her priorities were not academic but extracurricular. The teacher saw potential, and her casual attitude frustrated him. Mr. Anderson remained in education for only two years and left to become a Lutheran minister. Perhaps his priorities were not in order, since his power to influence one student fell on deaf ears.

CHAPTER 33

Commitment

Standing on your momma's porch, you told me that
you'd wait forever. And when you held my hand, I
knew that it was now or never. Those were the best days
of my life...back in the summer of sixty-nine.

—Summer of '69, Bryan Adams

THE HIGH SCHOOL YEARS BECAME a blur of activities. Russ and Lynn
continued to date, and the girl considered them a couple, while the
boy was not ready to commit. Even at such a young age, Lynn wondered, was she falling in love? Her heart said one thing. Yet her brain
and pride were reluctant to risk being hurt by this guy. Pathetically,
on Saturday afternoons, she waited by the telephone for him to call.
When the phone rang, she jumped to answer it, hoping Russ was
calling for a date. Sometimes, it was Russ; other times, the calls were
for her mother.

The Esko Class of '69 graduated in May, and Russ committed
to Bemidji State College and their basketball program. Both Russ
and Lynn took summer jobs, Russ with Minnesota Power and Lynn
worked at Rog's Galley, the local burger joint. Russ worked shifts
as a vacation replacement at the West Duluth steam power plant.
Lynn worked mostly afternoons from 5:00 p.m. to 11:00 p.m. with
her best friend Connie. When Russ finished his shift, he came to

the drive-in for a burger and fries. On occasion, Connie's boyfriend, Mark, showed up for a midnight snack, as well.

In spite of the girls feeding their boyfriends, the drive-in restaurant managed to net a healthy profit. The I-35 freeway wasn't constructed until five years later. Therefore, Highway 61 was the main thoroughfare from Duluth to the Twin Cities. Hungry travelers, buses filled with students, as well as, the locals often made their mealtime destination the little hamburger shack.

It was the summer of '69. Life for Russ and Lynn was carefree. Yet there was an underlying tension between the two, since Russ would leave very soon for college. Between work and baseball games, Russ had little free time to spend with Lynn, who wanted to go steady. She hoped to wear his class ring on her finger. He hoped he'd get a hit at his next baseball game.

For two weeks, Lynn didn't hear from Russ. He never called, and she feared a breakup was inevitable. Then, one day, Russ's mom called.

"Lynn, this is Jackie Davidson. I just wanted to let you know that Russ is in the hospital. He had his appendix removed yesterday."

Lynn gasped. "Is he going to be all right?"

"Russ should be released from St. Mary's Hospital in a few days."

"Can he have visitors?"

"Oh, sure, since you and Russ are 'friends,' I just wanted to let you know."

The conversation ended with a polite thank-you for calling. Then Lynn hung up the phone and began to cry.

Quickly, she made arrangements to drive to the hospital that same afternoon. When she entered room 425, Russ was sitting up in bed staring at the food tray.

His head lifted slightly to see Lynn smiling, yet her eyes were brimming with tears.

She came, she really cares, he thought, then attempted to be cool and drawled, "This hospital food sucks!"

Right then and there, Lynn knew that she loved that pale young man in the striped hospital gown. Russ told Lynn the ordeal of being rushed into surgery after vomiting blood. Fortunately, his appendix had not ruptured and a mother's quick thinking prevented serious complications for her son.

Although Russell's mother had been his first love, Jackie Davidson was not threatened by his friend. After all, her son had been dating this girl all during high school. Lynn had been to the house on many occasions. She seemed like a nice girl, who came from a good family. Eddy had known Lynn's parents practically all his life and the foursome had mutual friends.

Jackie's girlfriends warned her that Lynn was spoiled. But the girl had always been kind and respectful to her and Eddy. Lynn had even helped Russ babysit eight-year old son John and baby Joe.

Jackie hadn't seen Lynn recently and wondered if the relationship was cooling off since Russ was leaving soon for college. Yet, in her heart she knew that she must call Lynn to let her know about Russ's surgery. Just maybe he loved Lynn.

Hadn't she attempted to teach him the most important lesson of all – how to love, unconditionally…to show tenderness and compassion to others. For the time being, she was raising two teenage sons, as well as, two younger boys. Mothering four males presented quite a challenge especially after losing four day old daughter Debby, ten years earlier. How that loss crushed her spirit. But eventually the grief lifted when Johnny's birth filled the emptiness. Then five years later when Russ was a junior in high school, Jackie announced that she was going to have a baby. Russ' jaw nearly dropped to the kitchen floor as he thought "Whaaat? My parents are still having sex!" He did find solace in the fact that his good buddy Gerry's mom was expecting a child, too.

Jackie's all male household occasionally had a young female guest. Since Lynn hadn't been over for awhile, she wondered if her second son was no longer dating the Juntunen girl. But Jackie followed her heart and decided to call and mention that Russ had undergone an emergency appendectomy. Had she not listened to her instincts and God's still small voice within her, young love between her son and Lynn may have died.

But it didn't. And because she phoned Lynn, there was a turning point in the couple's relationship. The hospital visit proved to

Russ that Lynn really did care, and before he left for college, his class ring was on her finger.

Once Labor Day arrived, the young man packed his suitcase, a graduation gift from his girlfriend, and left for Bemidji State College. His roommate was an Esko classmate, Tom. The mothers made the three-hour drive, dropping off their sons and gear at the campus dorm room.

Jackie cried as she said, "Goodbye, Russ. Study hard, and call if you need anything."

The young man didn't understand why his mom was crying; he shrugged his shoulders and ran back to his new roost on the second floor of Oak Hall.

For the first six weeks, Russ participated in many student activities and purposely kept busy. Freshman orientation was rather boring, he thought. Still he'd met a few guys on his floor and at the gym. The campus was nestled along the scenic shore of Lake Bemidji, named by the Ojibwe tribe. A new dormitory, Oak Hall, with underground walking tunnels throughout the campus made every classroom accessible even during the cold harsh winter months. Cell phones or the Internet did not exist at the time. Communication was done by letter, and long-distance telephone calls, charged by the minute. One communal phone hung on the wall near the dorm stairwell. Most of the time, other guys had their ear to the receiver, which made it rarely available to Russ.

Much like Grandma Juntunen, who corresponded daily to her sons during World War II, Lynn began writing letters to her steady boyfriend. Every night, she sat on the soft chenille bedspread and penned a few lines telling him about life in Esko without him. Often, she dabbed perfume on the envelop. Between studying, mononucleosis, and ptomaine poisoning, Russ managed to write once a week.

If he wanted to get to Esko, Russell needed to find a ride since he didn't own a car. Toward the beginning of the third quarter, he was coming home just about every weekend. Sometimes in desperation, he hitchhiked the 145 miles just to be back in his hometown with Lynn and to feast on his mom's delicious home cooking.

About that same time during second semester, Russ and his roommate Tom committed to transfer to the University of Minnesota Duluth for their sophomore year. Both young men returned to Esko and lived at home with their parents. They carpooled the eighteen miles to the university and graduated with honors three years later.

The relationship between the two women in Russ' life continued to develop. Lynn became a student in Jackie's school of hospitality and entertaining. Much the same as in the girl's family, celebrating holidays became a high priority. The quote by Emily Griffin 'a son is a son 'til he gets a wife, but a daughter is a daughter all of her life' never materialized with Russ. Instead, the bond between mother and son remained steadfast while the bond between Jackie and Lynn grew stronger day by day. And eventually God blessed Jackie's male dominated family with three adoring granddaughters.

CHAPTER 34

Career Path

Know that wisdom is thus for your soul; If you find it, then there will be a future. And hope will not be cut off.
—Proverbs 24:14 (NASB)

TWO MEN PLAYED A MAJOR role in Lynn's career path. First, it was her father and his pragmatism which influenced her decision to attend a nine month beauty college in nearby Duluth. Neither parent was a four year college graduate and higher education for them seemed unnecessary. Therefore, they did not promote it.

Furthermore, Lynn witnessed their happiness and financial stability. As a traditional father, Ray assumed his daughter would never have to be the major bread winner; that would be a husband's responsibility, as it had been his.

Secondly, boyfriend Russell was committed to her. He loved Lynn and she knew ultimately they would marry. Consequently, practical economics navigated Lynn's course of action. She needed a trade, then a job to save money so the two high school sweethearts could marry.

Before graduation day the girl with the crooked bangs enrolled in the Duluth School of Cosmetology where she trained in cutting bangs and more. She decided to live with her parents to defray expenses, especially since Russ moved back home to Esko.

On the last Monday in August of 1970, Lynn drove the family sedan to downtown Duluth. Traffic was light for a Monday morning and Lynn was grateful.

Her mother had warned, "Don't drive too fast. If you leave by eight, you'll get there in plenty of time."

Mildred knew because she had driven the route seven years earlier while attending occupational therapy school in the Barnes Ames Building on Lake Avenue.

Amid the sultry morning, Lynn parked in the Second Avenue ramp, inhaled deeply, and stepped out from the '69 Chrysler Newport. Walking alone down Superior Street, the distinctive odor of ARCO coffee, roasted and marketed in Duluth, filled her nostrils combined with the exhaust from the city buses. She came to the stark realization that for the first time she would begin school without an entourage of her cousins and friends. As a result, the confident young woman grew apprehensive.

Entering the beauty school, Lynn joined a sea of white uniforms, who chatted together. She followed the hall signage to the office and registered with Ms. Donna. Lynn paid the first semester tuition with a check her mother wrote the night before scrawling in cursive "Mrs. Raymond Juntunen." Ms. Donna directed the new student to make her way to the lecture hall. Once there, she attempted to smile and exchange a few pleasantries with the other students. Lynn found herself in a new role. Instead of being a confident, high-profile senior, she was a timid unknown, freshman student.

For nine months, Lynn studied anatomy, Minnesota cosmetology rules and regulations, permanent waving, coloring, cutting, and styling of hair. She bonded with two freshmen girls, Cheryl and Doris, yet remained uncomfortable with the masses, almost shy.

A turning point occurred during the second semester of beauty school. The director, Mr. Pat, announced that a hairstyling competition would be held in two weeks. All students were encouraged to enter the contest. The girl with the crooked bangs never backed away from competition and signed up.

Immediately, Lynn decided that best friend Connie, must act as the model for the contest and later for state boards. Attractive Connie with her Italian ancestry, inherited wavy brunette locks, which were very easy to style.

From her experiences in past competitions, Lynn rose to the occasion and placed second among all the students. Three salon owners served as the judges. They, in turn, took notice of the winner and runner-up and recruited Lynn once she graduated in the spring.

Two interviews from two separate hair salons followed. Lynn chose to work at the shoppe in Cloquet simply because of the location. Her father's common sense left an indelible mark on Lynn. She reasoned that the commute to Cloquet could be made in ten minutes, while driving to Duluth would take twice as long with twice the traffic.

Furthermore, a fender bender three days later sealed her fate; she rear ended a car at the Fortieth and Grand Avenue stoplight.

Through tears, Lynn managed to drive back to Esko and face her father, who calmly reassured his daughter that it was just an accident; he was thankful she was all right.

"A car bumper can be replaced," Dad concluded, "but a person cannot."

Lynn hugged him and sobbed in his arms. What an understanding father she had.

Coincidentally, Russ's dad owned Eddy's Barber Shop on the corner of Fortieth and Grand. He witnessed the accident and mentioned the fact at the dinner table. "Hey Russ, this afternoon I saw that your girlfriend rear ended another car at the Grand Avenue stoplight. It looked like she was OK. I talked to the police officer and told him that I saw the accident from the barber shop…looked like a bruised front bumper."

Concerned, Russ jumped up from the table and grabbed the white phone hanging from the wall in the kitchen. He pulled the cord and himself up to the wooden staircase which lead to his bedroom upstairs. He shut the door for privacy.

"Hello, is Lynn there?" he asked Mildred.

"Ya, can she call you back?" was her reply.

"Sure, thanks," Russ said as he hung up the phone. He hated to call Lynn's house and have someone else answer other than Lynn. Nonetheless, he worried when his girlfriend drove by herself to school; there were some crazy driver's out there.

CHAPTER 35

Another Miracle

For you have rescued my soul from death. My eyes
from tears, my feet from stumbling. I shall walk
before the Lord in the land of the living.
—Psalm 116: 8–9 (NASB)

NURSES CONTINUED TO FUNNEL BACK *and forth into the intensive care
unit, while Russ slumped in the chair by the window. Absentmindedly, he
looked below and watched patrons on Third Street stumble into Loisel's
Liquor Store. People went about their day-to-day business while Russ's
life stood still. His daughters entered the unit one at a time and stared
at their mother lying motionless in the hospital bed. Three hours crept by
before a doctor stepped in.*

*"What is going on? Lynn is not responding at all!" the strained
husband demanded.*

*"Let me explain," the doctor spelled out. "We know Lynn's sodium
levels are dangerously low. We must be very careful restoring her electro-
lytes to a normal level. Her organs could be compromised and that might
be catastrophic. It's apparent that the swelling in her brain is receding
because she's not grabbing her head anymore. Please know that we are
doing everything possible for your wife."*

"Okay, how long might this take?"

*"We don't know," Dr. Blinn said, "every person is different. Let's
just wait and see what happens."*

As the doctor left the sterile cubicle, Russ thought, "Wait and see," that's all we've been doing—WAITING. *Seven hours had passed since that fateful phone call. His eyes shot up to the clock above the bed where his wife lay motionless. It showed four o'clock.*

Just then, there was a light knock on the glass enclosure. "May I come in?" Father Walsh quietly asked.

He was the parish priest who had recently returned from Ireland.

"I found out that Lynn was in a car accident. I've been away, unable to make hospital visits. How is she doing?"

Russ's despondent eyes said it all as he responded, "Lynn may not know you. She's been staring into space, not recognizing any of us. But why don't you say a prayer for her and for us?"

Father Walsh placed his hand on Lynn's arm and began to pray. She slowly opened her eyes and said, "Well, hello, Father Walsh!"

Russ gasped and began to cry. Lynn looked at her sobbing husband, exclaiming, "What's the matter with you?"

Tears of relief and joy began to flood over Russ as he laughed and then cried again at the sound of his wife's voice.

He didn't attempt explaining to Lynn what had transpired. Instead, Russ made a beeline to the intensive care waiting area to find his daughters and tell them the good news. Their mother was awake, talking, and feisty.

CHAPTER 36

A New Plan

For I know the plans I have for you, a plan to prosper you
and not harm you. A plan to give you hope and a future.
—Jeremiah 29:11 (NIV)

FOLLOWING GRADUATION FROM THE DULUTH School of Cosmetology
in June of '71, Lynn opted to work in Cloquet at the Red Carpet
Boutique, instead of Duluth at Rosemary's Carousel. Two women,
Caroline and Joyce, co-owned the business on Cloquet Avenue. One
was a hairstylist, and the other was a makeup specialist and savvy
businesswoman. Both women sold the very popular synthetic wigs
and hairpieces, but only Caroline could trim them to custom fit each
patron.

The two women decided to expand into a full-service salon and
needed a fresh young stylist. Lynn was hired, and under their tutelage, she was taught business and marketing 101. Weekly newspaper ads announced the addition of a new hairstylist, and Lynn hit
the floor running. The long hot summer proved stifling in the small
quarters that were not air-conditioned. The stench from permanent
wave solution permeated the salon's air, but Lynn didn't mind. She
was gainfully employed, making money, secretly wondering whether
she and Russ could perhaps marry within a year.

The beauty shop was doing so well that an additional stylist was
hired. Three stations separated by half walls were decorated in rich

reds with black and gold accents…very seventies style. Whenever possible, Lynn walked next door to the Coney Island for lunch. The down-home cooking at the restaurant was delicious, and Lynn discovered that her stylish new uniforms were fitting rather snuggly. She decided to start eating salads instead of the burgers and fries she'd been wolfing down in-between clients.

When she missed her period in July, Lynn drove to the Raiter Clinic to take a pregnancy test. Accurate home digital tests were not yet available to the general public. Later in the afternoon her family doctor called the beauty shop and asked for Lynn, who found privacy in the back room where she could talk.

She took hold of the receiver, placed it to her ear, and heard the words, "Your test came back positive. Why don't you call back in a few weeks to make a follow-up appointment?"

"Okay, thanks," Lynn said barely audible.

Then she carefully hung up the telephone and looked at Caroline, who quickly walked over and gave the rookie employee a long hug.

It was a Friday, and Russ planned to see Lynn after he finished working the afternoon shift at the steam plant. The temperature in the boiler room must've been over one hundred degrees, and he stunk sweat. Still, he sensed that Lynn's voice sounded a bit strange when he called during his break. Without showering, he drove his little red Volkswagen straight from the plant to her house.

Lynn took the time before Russ arrived to formulate a plan. She knew they'd marry just as soon as arrangements could be made. After all, they loved each other. Of course, a few details needed adjustment.

Before Russ stepped out from the red Beetle, Lynn was waiting and met him at his car door. She wanted to be quiet since Millie and Ray were asleep in the house.

The night air was humid, and the sky dark with clouds. The two sat side by side in the little car, and without hesitation, Lynn began the conversation.

"I found out today that I'm pregnant." She paused, and when Russ remained speechless, Lynn continued, "So we'll get married sooner than we thought. I told my mom, and she talked to Dad. I just couldn't face him. I thought that I had disappointed him. Instead of showing disappointment, my dad said that we can live here at their house until you finish college."

"We can't take advantage of your parents," retorted Russ.

"My dad, much like his father, takes care of his own," Lynn explained. "Many of my aunts and uncles after marrying lived at the farm for a while. They worked and saved money, and then Pa helped them find or build houses. This is nothing new for my dad or grandpa. They always help out their family. That's just what they do, and someday so will we."

It's been said that a daughter needs a dad to be the standard against which she will judge all men. She knew in her heart that Russ was a good man; he was honest, smart, and loyal. He measured up to those high standards.

She remembered the quote, "Fathers, be your daughters first love, and she'll never settle for anything less."

And so it was for this young couple; they would be given free lodging in the Juntunen basement apartment until Russ graduated from college. This generous act kept the young couple out of debt until they bought their home on Memorial Drive.

A father's love for his daughter knows no limits. It was true for Ray and his little girl with the crooked bangs. Those words would become a reality for Russell when three daughters captured his forever love.

CHAPTER 37

A Wonderful Wedding Gift

> For I am fearfully and wonderfully made. My
> frame was not hidden from you.
> —Psalm 139: 14–15 (NASB)

A BABY IS A GIFT from God, an extraordinary miracle, which happens every day to women around the world.

The little girl with the crooked bangs was getting married. Her dream wedding was scaled down considerably, because she was old-fashioned. She blamed herself for getting pregnant, but Lynn was always the hardest on herself.

For twenty years, Lynn gained much attention from an array of accomplishments. She sang and cheered and directed and won. She enjoyed all the fanfare. Despite that, these accomplishments had swollen her heart with a dangerous pride. Becoming pregnant before marriage jolted Lynn off her high horse and gave her a dose of reality.

Fortunately, she learned in Sunday school that God does not make mistakes. He makes miracles. Lynn believed that every child conceived was a miracle.

She believed that sometimes there aren't words for the most amazing things that happen in our lives, for miracles that could only be gifts from heaven. Little did Lynn know that becoming a mother would set her life on a different trajectory for actualizing her greatest blessings…three daughters.

Her first miracle of life was slowly developing underneath the wedding gown that she carefully slipped over her head. The dress was purchased at the same bridal shop in Duluth where she was fitted for her first prom dress only four years earlier. The fabric was white taffeta and billowed into an empire waist with sheer sleeves. Thin pink ribbon threaded through the bodice and hemline. Lynn's fingers slowly ran across the fine fabric lightly touching her tummy. Then after making a final adjustment to the shoulder length veil, she peered into the mirror and smiled with approval. The wedding dress was simple yet tasteful.

The noon wedding was held at St. Casimir's Catholic Church with the immediate family in attendance. Lynn's sister Janet was the matron of honor, while Russ's older brother Dick served as best man. He wore a hunting vest under his tuxedo for a special touch of humor. Instead of participating in the duck-hunting opener, he was attending his brother's shotgun wedding. The mother of the bride sewed a pink floor-length bridesmaid dress for Janet, who carried a bouquet of pink roses.

The nineteen-year-old daughter walked into the church vestibule where her parents waited. Lynn's eyes met her mother's, and tears began to trickle down her cheek.

Mildred attempted to console her daughter by saying, "Now don't cry, Lynn. Everything is gonna be all right. Be strong now."

Next she handed the young bride a small white Bible graced with white tea roses and trailing stephanotis.

Lynn gulped and took her father's big strong arm. Raymond slowly walked his "baby" down the aisle of the unfamiliar church. Because Russ was Catholic, Lynn agreed to be married in his church. During the couple's premarriage classes, she reluctantly signed an affidavit consenting to raise in the Catholic faith any children conceived by the couple. Sadly, ignorance and narrow-mindedness contributed to the young woman's judgmental attitude. In the latter years, her faith would grow deeper because of this decision.

However, on that October wedding day, Lynn's Lutheran family sat quietly in the church pew not quite understanding the foreign Roman Catholic liturgy. They watched as their little girl with crooked bangs stood facing an altar where on the back wall a replica of Jesus hung on a large cross.

After a greeting and three scripture readings, the groom carefully repeated his vows to the bride. Then it was Lynn's turn.

As he looked to the bride, the priest said, "Repeat these words after me."

Since Lynn hadn't stopped crying during the ceremony, she shook her head and whispered, "I can't."

Russ looked at her and thought, *She's backing out. She's not going to marry me.*

Despite the slight delay, Russ was mistaken. Lynn choked through her vows to the groom, and then the priest exclaimed, "I now pronounce you man and wife. Go in peace to love and serve the Lord. You may kiss the bride!"

When the ceremony concluded, those in attendance gathered at the Davidson's house. Mother Jackie prepared a roast beef dinner with all the trimmings. Three hours later, a reception for 250 guests was held at Lynn's family church in Esko. Chicken salad, rolls, and cake were served by the ladies' group. A wedding dance followed at the Proctor Village Hall, where a live band played polka music.

The exhausted bride and groom left the dance by 11:00 p.m., but the wedding guests' revelry continued well into the early morning hours. Russ reserved a lakeside room at the newly built Radisson hotel in downtown Duluth. The couple collapsed on the king-size bed and slept soundly until daylight.

Russ woke up first and slightly opened the heavy brocade draperies only to see concrete, the St. Louis County jail, and courthouse. Instead of getting a room overlooking the Lake Superior harbor, the newlyweds were given a room facing the Duluth hillside where cars careened up and down Mesaba Avenue. They laughed about the mix-up and the fact that they hadn't noticed until morning.

After checking out of the hotel by 1:00 p.m., Russ and Lynn went back home to open their wedding gifts and cards. No romantic honeymoon followed on account of Russ's calculus test slated for Monday afternoon. Rather on Sunday night, a Sonny and Cher concert at the Duluth Arena Auditorium temporarily fulfilled that obligation. Unfortunately, Cher was experiencing vocal or perhaps marital trauma. As a result, Sonny yodeled many of their hit songs, and the live concert was a minor disappointment.

Even so, the weekend went off without a major hitch. The bride and groom were gifted with beautiful china, small household appliances, linens and bedding, all which were carefully packed away until the couple moved into their own place. Friends and family were also very generous with monetary gifts, which sustained them during the months Russ attended college and while Lynn worked at the Red Carpet Hair Salon. The two never forgot the generosity shown to them on their wedding day and vowed to give likewise unto others.

To close out the wedding weekend, Russ and Lynn made their way back to Esko and the Juntunen home. The two tiptoed down the basement steps not wanting to wake Lynn's parents, who were already asleep in their bedroom on the main floor. The past three days had drained them all. For this reason, sleep softly and sweetly beckoned the newly married couple nestled side by side on the sofa sleeper in the basement family room.

CHAPTER 38

Healing

But I will restore you to health and heal your wounds.
—Jeremiah 30:17 (NIV)

ONCE LYNN STABILIZED AFTER THE *sodium fiasco, surgery to rod the broken femur was rescheduled for Thursday, that is if Lynn continued to make progress. Still Dr. Boman was concerned that a blood clot might form near the site of the break and travel to her heart or lung. Considering Lynn's fragile state, it could kill her.*

Several doctors examined Lynn to determine whether the orthopedic surgeon could operate. By 7:00 a.m., she was cleared for surgery. Russ drove to the hospital, getting to Lynn's room a half hour later. Other family members began to filter into the surgical waiting area, only to be forced to sit and wait once again. Finally, Lynn was taken into surgery at 2:00 p.m.

Russ sat alone with his thoughts and never once relayed to his daughters or to Lynn's parents and sister Janet just how critical the surgery might be. Dr. Boman had warned Russ that putting Lynn under anesthesia after the sodium scare was risky. Yet leaving the broken femur unattended could prove disastrous.

Jackie walked with her son to the hospital café. She sensed his worry and hoped food would help ease Russ' nerves. She was the typical "Polish momma." Didn't good food cure everything? Yet food was not the cure-all that day. Russ hung his head and barely swallowed a morsel.

"Lynn's going to be just fine, Russ," the mother soothed.

"Mom, it's more complicated than what I'm sharing with the girls. This surgery is very, very serious because of her blood issues. Lynn could die!"

Once again, prayers echoed the hospital corridors, as well as homes across America. Hundreds of faith-filled friends and family interceded for Lynn. Two and a half hours slowly passed, when Dr. Boman strutted into the waiting area and told everyone that the rodding was successful. Robyn, Brooke, and Amy ran up to the surgeon still wearing blue scrubs. They formed a circle and hugged the man while crying in sync.

The good-natured doctor joked, "I usually don't get quite this warm reaction from a patient's family!"

Relieved and exhausted most of the family made their way home. Russ waited until his wife was wheeled back into ICU. Then he tenderly kissed her cheek and left the hospital. Seemed like he'd practically been living there for the past two weeks. How he wished that lady Grace hadn't slammed into his wife's van.

As it was, the next morning, Lynn transferred from the ICU to the fourth floor. Visitors were restricted to immediate family only, and nurses became bouncers policing the well intended. Janet came to the hospital every day despite her own health problems. Often Jackie accompanied her for short visits. Robyn returned to work in Roseville, and her sisters went back to school.

Lynn's temperament mellowed with IV pain medication and she was humbled by all the love and concern that she was shown.

Avon Corporation and their insurance provider hired a case worker to oversee Lynn's recovery. A meeting took place among hospital staff and personnel to insure Lynn was receiving optimum health care and to establish a time line for the patient.

A barrage of therapists forced Lynn to move her broken body and strengthen muscles that had been idle for days. In particular, she could not eat independently and required assistance at mealtime and toileting.

The long cast on the right leg was beginning to itch; Lynn wanted to take a shower alone and couldn't. The right hand flopped down. No matter how hard she tried, Lynn could not lift it up. As a result, she attempted to train her feeble left hand to grip a pen or comb. This only frustrated her.

A neurologist, Dr. Young, performed several minor tests to evaluate sensory response in the right arm. He suggested a follow-up in April of electromyography to explore radial nerve function.

Lynn felt powerless and vulnerable. Nonetheless, "sisu" enabled her to push onward through the torture of rehab. She was determined to get back on her feet again and set a goal to walk for Brooke's high school graduation on May 27.

At long last, Russ returned to school along with Brooke and Amy. The trio attempted to regain some normalcy in their lives but found it difficult to concentrate. Their emotions were raw and frayed. Time to recover was needed for everyone involved.

CHAPTER 39

We Can Stay

You will be blessed when you come in and blessed when you go out.
—Deuteronomy 28:6 (NIV)

DURING FIRST QUARTER OF RUSS'S senior year at UMD, he requested to do his student teaching at Independent School District 99. Mr. Elton Waterhouse was retiring at the end of the school year. A position would open in the Esko math department. In the meantime, the college student kept studying and maintaining a GPA of 3.8 in spite of difficult upper division courses.

Before the first quarter finals, Russ was informed by his advisor that his request had been granted. He was to report in Esko to Mr. Waterhouse's classroom after Christmas break. Once there, he had to prove himself as the person who would be worthy to replace a seasoned, successful pro. Clearly, these were huge shoes to fill, yet Russ never backed down from a challenge and knew exactly what he had to do.

The Christmas holiday arrived, and the New Year was filled with renewed hope. Classes for Esko students resumed on January 8. Russ dressed carefully that first morning, putting on a tan corduroy sport coat, white dress shirt and navy blue tie. He arrived at the school before 7:15 a.m. but wasn't surprised to see his mentor already in room 206. Mr. Waterhouse was seated at his desk finalizing lesson plans. He glanced up and smiled as his former student entered.

"Good morning, Russell."

"Good morning, Mr. Waterhouse."

"Are you all ready to become a teacher?"

"Yes, I am."

"I will have you sit in the back of the class and observe for a week or two. Then I expect you can take over the class."

"Okay, Mr. Waterhouse," Russ answered and glanced over to the doorway.

Students slowly filtered into the room, unhappy that their Christmas break was over yet pleasantly surprised to see a younger man with Mr. Waterhouse.

The student teacher studied the seventh-grade textbook pretending not to notice the girls walking by and snickering. He thought, *Oh, boy, I will be dealing with giggling junior high girls for the next semester.*

Unbeknown to Russ, he'd be dealing with three giggling daughters before the '70s decade ended. In the meantime, Russ knew that he needed to learn the art of making math appealing to both male and female students.

Once the school bell rang, Mr. Waterhouse introduced Russ. "Class, this is Mr. Davidson, who once sat in this very same classroom. He will be your student teacher until the end of the school year. Please show him the respect you show me. Now who's absent this first day back to school?"

Then after taking roll, Mr. Waterhouse told the class to open their books to chapter 12.

The weeks passed by, and Elton Waterhouse mentored his student teacher, who swallowed every morsel that he was fed. The master teacher emphasized the three *F*s: Be Firm, Be Friendly, Be Fair.

Russell listened, learned, and later asked for a recommendation. Mr. Waterhouse wholeheartedly supported this young instructor and recommended that the administration hire Russell Davidson as his replacement. Russell interviewed with Dr. Hanson, the superintendent, who fell asleep during the interview. The man suffered with narcolepsy of which Russ was unaware. Instead, the novice teacher thought for sure his answers in the interview were so boring that the man fell asleep! All things considered, the superintendent offered Russ a full-time math position at Esko. He slid the contract across his desk for the young man to look over during the weekend.

Overjoyed and relieved, Russ rushed home to tell Lynn. He forgot it was Friday, and she was working at the salon. He called the Red Carpet anyway and asked for his wife to come to the phone.

Sally, the receptionist, waved Lynn from the back shampoo station to take the call.

Russ calmly spoke, "I got the job, Lynn."

"Oh myyyy," Lynn cried out, "now we don't have to move away from our families!"

"That's right."

"We can talk more once I finish here and come home."

Lynn hung up the phone and attempted tearfully to explain that Russ was hired as the junior high math teacher at Esko. Sally, knowing just how much this meant to the couple, tightly hugged Lynn as the two women joyfully jumped up and down.

When the last client left the beauty shop pleased with her new Dorothy Hamil haircut, Lynn quickly cleaned up her station and drove home. She arrived to find a house full of people, who were already celebrating.

Finally, the long hours studying to earn a college degree paid off for Russ. He was going to teach and coach next September at his alma mater. Preparation would have to wait. For now, Russ needed to raise a glass and toast the man who was instrumental in the hire, his mentor...Mr. Elton Waterhouse.

As fate would have it, two weeks before school dismissed for the summer, Mr. Waterhouse developed severe chest pains. Doctors advised him to stay home and rest. Reluctantly, he agreed and wanted his student teacher to fill in as the substitute for the remainder of the school year. Mr. Waterhouse reasoned with the principal that Russ was familiar with the current curriculum, the students, and already had been hired to replace him in September.

Consequently, Mr. Davidson finished out the school year for Mr. Waterhouse. Still, Russ missed the little man with a big heart, who became a trusted friend and advisor. To commemorate the bond between the two men, Russ brought a box of chocolates to Mr. Waterhouse every Christmas Eve for the next ten years. The young man shared with the older man his classroom successes and foibles. When Elton passed away, his family asked Russell to give the eulogy at the funeral. He was honored and humbly accepted.

*****

Finally, the time had come for Lynn and Russ to move from their basement apartment...but not very far. A person in the United States is expected to move 11.4 times in his lifetime. Even so, the little girl with the crooked bangs moved only three times and never strayed too far from Joseph and Elsa's homestead along the Midway River.

Since the new teacher signed his first contract with the Esko school district, he and his wife needed a place to live with two-year-old Robyn. Great-aunt Mamie owned a two-bedroom mobile home that rented for thirty-five dollars a month. It was located about two hundred yards north of Ray and Millie's house and was available. So the couple moved in June without signing a rental agreement or giving the lender a deposit. Mamie trusted family, and Lynn understood this privilege was not to be taken lightly.

When the winter wind began to howl through the gigantic fir trees, Russ tucked extra insulation around the trailer's skirting. The exterior walls and floor were cold, and a draft scooted along the floor like a mouse being chased by a barn cat. During the chilly nights, the inefficient gas furnace rarely shut down. Since the bedrooms were on opposite ends of the trailer, hearing a toddler's cry above the blower on the heating system was virtually impossible. The situation prompted the couple to look for a house to purchase in the Esko area.

A cozy three-bedroom cottage with a breezeway to the garage was in their price range. Russ asked his dad Ed to take a look since he didn't know much about home construction. Lynn liked the house and wanted to buy it. Ed said it was poorly built. Lynn looked at the esthetics, while her father-in-law was more pragmatic and looked at the bones of the structure. In the end, they didn't buy the cute little house on Helberg Road.

Instead only days later, another house came onto the market. A three-bedroom rambler about ten years old was for sale. The house had a fireplace, unfinished basement, and was only two blocks from the school. The house next door was owned by Lynn's uncle and aunt, Howard and Inga. Location, location, location screamed, "Buy me. Buy me. Buy me!"

Needless to say, another interested party had already placed an offer on the house. Russ, trusting a friend's wise advice, suspected what that offer might be and had an earnest money contract drawn up for one hundred dollars more than the guesstimate. Several other advantages factored in to the deal. The contract was not contingent on the buyer's need to sell a house, as was the case with the first offer. Also, the sellers were relocating to Indiana and desperate to move quickly.

The amazed realtor jokingly told Russ, "You must've been looking through the paperwork on my desk."

"No, Roger." Russ grinned as he added, "I may have a way with numbers and a very savvy friend."

The deal was finalized one month later and Russ, Lynn and two-year old Robyn moved in to the rambler on Eight Memorial Drive. A volunteer crew of Ray, Millie, Betty, and Jackie painted every room in the house. The excited little family finally had a place of their own. Lynn used her personal savings, i.e., money from birthdays, and high school graduation, for the down payment of $3,000. An additional $1,000 was allocated for new harvest gold Kenmore appliances including a washer, dryer, stove, and refrigerator.

Life was good and they could stay.

CHAPTER 40

There's No Place Like Home

We went through fire and water, but you brought
us back to a place of abundance.

—Psalm 66:12 (NIV)

*THE GOOD NEWS WAS THAT, Lynn was going to be released from a twen-
ty-day hospital stay. The bad news was that the house on Memorial Drive
was not ready for her return. Doctors wrote orders for Rxs, in home therapy, and follow-up appointments. Nurses attempted to draw up all the
necessary paperwork. The insurance liaison representative coordinated all
of the arrangements.*

*Meanwhile, on the home front, Danny constructed a wheelchair
ramp for the front entrance and installed a second phone line. Then
he, Jackie, Ray, and nephew Tom painted the living room only after
Brooke's football buddies moved the sofa into the lower-level family room.
Additional space was needed for a hospital bed to be placed in the front
living room. Millie washed clothes, and Janet cleaned until everything
was spic and span. Later in the afternoon, a wheelchair and commode
were delivered from Midwest Medical Supply.*

*The patient was released from St. Mary's and was loaded into the
Med-A-Van. All of a sudden, fear gripped Lynn as she stared motionless
at the back of driver's head. She hadn't ridden in a vehicle since the accident. She felt weak and light-headed, but what was she to do? The van*

and its driver were the only transportation home. And surely she wanted to go home.

After closing her eyes the majority of the ride south along I-35, the passenger relaxed slightly as the familiar surroundings of Thomson Township came into view. Most of winter's snow had melted since February 8. Still there were plenty of reminders that spring had not yet sprung.

Nine family members waited patiently for the patient to arrive. Finally, the van pulled into the Davidson driveway, and its driver got out. He opened the cargo door to reveal their precious cargo.

Everyone cheered while the driver pushed the wheelchair up the ramp and into the house. Tears rolled down her cheeks as Lynn looked around the freshly painted living room, a hospital bed now in place of a sofa, flowers on every table, and a banner spelling, "Welcome Home."

Much like Dorothy from the Wizard of Oz, Lynn knew in her heart, "there's no place like home."

The hospital bed faced large casement windows giving Lynn a grand view of the front yard and giving everyone else immediate access to her. The house had a revolving door with people coming in and out.

Home health care staff and nurses provided their services twenty-four hours a day. The Esko community showered Lynn and her family with love and food. Greeting cards and packages continued to arrive at the nearby post office. The Esko teachers generously supplied the family with home-cooked meals for an entire month. Pastors from the Esko churches stopped by for short visits. Physical and occupational therapists called on Lynn three times a week.

Recovery was a slow process. Lynn slept for three weeks in the hospital bed. One night, she needed assistance to get onto her commode to pee. The nurse had fallen asleep in the lower-level family room and did not hear the monitor's beep for help. Lynn was desperate but didn't want to yell and wake up a sleeping family. Hadn't they been through enough? And, besides, they all had school in the morning. So very slowly, Lynn shimmied off the sheets and, while balancing on one leg, dropped her body onto the commode.

"Ahhh, finally relief," she whispered to herself. Yet just as beadlets of sweat formed on her face, she realized just how weak she was and still

had to push herself back onto the hospital bed. Lynn hated the fact that she was so frail and dependent on others.

Meanwhile, the next day, furious Russ fired the night nurse. As a result, Lynn returned to the master bedroom where she slept nights next to her protecting husband's side.

Lynn was determined to free herself from the wheelchair and walk for Brooke's high school graduation. With her husband on her arm, she did. Brooke delivered a heartfelt speech recalling her role as Dorothy from the Wizard of Oz which she had portrayed years earlier in an elementary program. Clicking her heels together she exclaimed, "There's no place like home!" Cheers followed the ceremony that concluded with the All-Night Post-Grad Party.

*****

One week later, two hundred family members and friends honored Brooke by attending her graduation party at the house. Janet coordinated the event, while Lynn stood with Brooke on the front steps, hugging and welcoming guests. The day of celebration marked the end of Brooke's high school career and the beginning of a new phase as a college coed. Also, the day was a celebration of new life…beginning again. Death valiantly tried to destroy the Davidson family unit and take its wife and mother, but that was not to be.

CHAPTER 41

Three Little Women

I do think that families are the most
beautiful things in all the world.
—Little Women, Louisa May Alcott

ONCE RUSS AND LYNN SETTLED into their new home, the couple decided that it was time for the stork to bring Robyn a baby sister or brother. A year later, Russ's second cheerleader slid down the birth canal as Lynn's water broke at the same time she was bearing down and pushing. This phenomenon is sometimes referred to as a "wet birth." Brooke Rae was named after Meadowbrook Dairy and her grandpa Ray, who was part owner in the family corporation.

During the nine-month pregnancy, Lynn wondered if she could love another child as much as she loved Robyn, her firstborn. Yet the moment she held Brooke Rae in her arms, she knew. Mother love deepened as Lynn understood that each beautiful child is unique and special with their own personality and gifts. How precious every child is in the eyes of the Lord.

About the same time Lynn was giving birth to babies, her spirit was searching for a rebirth, as well. Cousin Anne and her husband, Jeff, moved next door to Lynn's parents. She invited Lynn, Janet, and their mother to join a Bible study. Anne left a lasting imprint on all three women, as they recommitted their lives to Christ.

In the beginning, Lynn thought she could work through most challenges by her own strength and determination. This belief was a bold lie from Satan himself, who knew Lynn's prideful heart.

The young woman realized her inadequacies and learned that being a good mother required seeking the fruits of the Spirit: unconditional love, joy, peace, patience, goodness, kindness, and self-control. These attributes developed first, by recognizing the need, by putting pride and ego aside and submitting to the Holy Spirit.

In the past, the young woman mistakenly thought she could control her destiny by being good and working hard. How wrong she'd been. Instead while attending Anne's Bible study, the basic lessons of faith and grace that she learned as a child were reinforced. She did not have to "go it alone." Lynn could lean on a "Higher Power" to help her in the most important role she'd ever encounter… motherhood.

Two years passed, and the Davidson household was energized by two little girls. Russ was teaching, coaching, and being pulled in many directions. Along with homemaking, Lynn styled hair three days a week at the Red Carpet. She wanted to spend as much time as possible with her daughters. Before long, they'd both be all day in school.

One chilly November night, Russ and Lynn had a candid discussion. The family had just celebrated Russ's birthday with a lasagna dinner, Caesar salad, crusty bread, and a black forest chocolate cake for dessert. The kids were bathed, in bed, and tired after their daddy's celebration. The girls loved when Mommy hosted parties, especially when their grandparents came over.

But now the house was quiet, the guests gone, the girls asleep. Lynn began the conversation.

"Do you want to have any more kids, Russ?"

"I dunno. How do you feel about another baby?" he asked.

"I'm not sure what we should do," Lynn replied. The intrauterine device (IUD) as birth control was causing discomfort and needed to be removed. Her second pregnancy had been more difficult, and varicose veins in the right leg and groin bulged and occasionally throbbed.

"I'll make an appointment tomorrow with Dr. Albertson and talk with him."

One week later, Lynn was at the clinic visiting her doctor. They discussed alternate forms of birth control. Unfortunately, the IUD was lodged and could not be removed during the clinic visit. For this reason, Lynn had to have the device surgically extracted at the hospital. She returned two days later as a follow-up to the procedure. Since Lynn hadn't decided whether or not she'd have a third child, she was given a monthly supply of birth control pills for the time being. Once the Christmas holiday was over, the couple would make a decision whether they'd try to get pregnant.

New Year's Eve was celebrated with a party at cousin Craig and his wife Judy's house. The two couples had continued their friendship that began when they first dated in high school. Now each had two children. For health reasons, Russ and Lynn decided not to have any more children.

The year of 1978 began, and school resumed after the Christmas break. Robyn was in kindergarten and loved to share family stories at "show-and-tell." One frigid January day, she told her teacher, Mrs. Lindstrom, that her mommy was going to have a baby. The little girl wanted to share a sensational story.

Clearly, the topic of trying to conceive another child was never discussed with "the girls," who were now five and three years old. Maybe just maybe, Robyn "knew" more than her parents, who had scheduled a tubal ligation for February 1.

This procedure was a permanent sterilization, cauterizing a woman's Fallopian tubes, and at that time, required the consent of both the husband and the wife. On the first day of the month, Russ drove his wife to the Cloquet hospital where only a few years earlier Lynn had given birth to both Robyn and Brooke.

He asked once again, "Are you sure you want to do this?"

"Yes, I am. God has blessed us with two healthy daughters," Lynn said. "I don't want to risk another pregnancy since I'm taking Dilantin and Mysoline to control seizures.

Six years earlier, while in high school, Lynn experienced symptoms of fainting, feelings of déjà vu, and zoning out. As a result, she was diagnosed with petit mal epilepsy after undergoing several tests including an EEG (electroencephalogram).

Dr. Albertson consulted with a neurologist, who prescribed low dosages of the antiseizure drugs. The medications worked so effectively that Lynn had no restrictions. Unfortunately, there were risks if taking them during pregnancy. Possibly a child could be born with the birth defect of a cleft palate or a seizure disorder.

Lynn rested comfortably after the tubal ligation and was preparing to go home when the doctor stepped into her room on the second floor.

He cleared his throat, looked down, and slowly began to speak, "Ahhh, the surgery went well, and you may have some cramping. I want to run a urine test. Your uterus appeared thick and larger than usual. You may be pregnant."

Before the physician left the hospital to begin a full afternoon seeing patients at the Raiter Clinic, he telephoned the lab to get the results of Mrs. Davidson's test. Just as he suspected, she was about three weeks pregnant. He scolded himself for not getting a urine specimen before the surgery. According to his patient, she hadn't experienced any signs indicating she was pregnant. Now he must break the news that she was with child. Although Lynn and her husband had signed a document giving permission for sterilization, a very small fetus was living within the woman's uterus.

The doctor slowly walked down the long hallway to room 224 and pushed open the heavy door. Glancing upward, he saw Lynn sitting on the hospital bed, awaiting the doctor's discharge orders. Already dressed in street clothes, the young woman was anxious to get back home before the school bus dropped off Robyn.

Sheepishly, he muttered, "The test came back as we suspected. You're pregnant."

He waited for Lynn's response who was speechless for the moment. So he continued, never making eye contact, "Since you and Russ signed the document for sterilization, if you want to abort the pregnancy, I can make the arrangements."

Stunned by what was happening, Lynn emphatically retorted, "Oh no, Doctor, my husband and I were not sure if we should have another child. Although we thought one way, God had another plan. This baby growing in my womb is destined to be a part of our little family."

Eight months later, Amy Lynn arrived at 6:00 a.m. on September 18, her uncle Joe's birthday. Dr. Albertson invited Russ to watch the delivery, but Russ misunderstood the physician's invitation and pulled his wristwatch off to give it to the doctor. "No, no!" the doc exclaimed. "Do you want to watch?"

Recently, a new policy had been adopted, allowing fathers the opportunity to share in the birthing experience. Russ wanted no part of it. He jumped to his feet, quickly declined the offer, then nervously sat back in his chair.

Two days later, Mommy and baby came home. Both Robyn and Brooke were waiting with Grandma Jackie at the door to meet their sister. It's been said that children are keen observers. Eight months earlier, Robyn told the kindergarten teacher and the entire class that her mommy was having a baby. It was during "show-and-tell." Robyn thought it would be a great story to share. Or perhaps God whispered to the little five-year-old with the long blonde curls. Whatever the case, a third Davidson girl consummated the family unit.

Three little women completed Russ's harem. Surprisingly, this guy reared in his parents' home with three brothers now resided with an all-female ménage. Even the cat was a girl. All the same, he adjusted quite nicely, and with each passing day, he grew to love them more and more.

Ten months after Amy's birth, Lynn attended a prayer meeting. She listened intently to the speaker, who shared the bible story from Matthew 9 about the young girl, who suffered for twelve years with a bleeding disorder. She heard of this man Jesus, who performed miracles and hoped he might help her when he came to town. Throngs of people crowded the square. The girl attempted to get close to Jesus. She believed He had the power to heal. All she could do was merely touch the hem of his garment. Instantly, the bleeding subsided. Jesus said that her faith had made her well.

Once the speaker's testimony ended, she invited people to come to the front for prayer. Lynn sensed a nudging in her spirit and cautiously stepped forward. She explained how at eighteen she was diagnosed with petit mal epilepsy and took anti-seizure medications. The woman placed her hand on Lynn's forehead and asked God to heal her of the neurological disorder. The speaker acted as a channel for supernatural healing. After the prayer meeting, Lynn discontinued the seizure prescriptions (not recommended for everyone). She believed God for a complete healing and never experienced another petit mal seizure.

The young mother did not fully understand why epilepsy was no longer an affliction. Yet, by childlike faith much like the girl with the bleeding disorder, Lynn stepped forward at the prayer meeting and was healed.

The Son of Righteousness shall rise with healing in his wings. Malachi 4:2, NASB.

CHAPTER 42

Recovering, One Step at a Time

The thief comes only to steal, and kill, and destroy;
I have come that you may have life and have it abundantly.
—John 10:10 (NASB)

IN SPITE OF HER OWN *personal health issues, Janet became the calming voice and helper during Lynn's long recovery. She visited the hospital just about every day, making sure her younger sister was receiving the best care. She was a quiet shoulder for the girls to lean on. One time in the hospital waiting room, Robyn hugged Auntie Jan Jan and admitted, "You smell like my mom." This brought tears to both of them as they considered the fact that Lynn's life had been spared.*

When Lynn's sodium level dropped and she was in critical condition, Janet gave Robyn, Brooke, and Amy index cards. On the cards were handwritten Bible verses:

"Trust in the Lord with all your heart, lean not unto your own understanding. Fear not, for I AM with you. No weapon formed against you will prosper. For you have rescued my soul from death."

The girls kept the cards close by. When scared or troubled, they pulled them from their pockets and read over and over again the comforting script. Lynn's daughters memorized and claimed those Bible verses.

Janet also began a daily diary to chronicle the hospital happenings. Visitors or patients' orders were methodically penned on a simple yellow lined tablet. This tablet became invaluable later to Lynn, who couldn't remember most of the events. Journaling a timetable kept the days and events from running together in a blur.

Lynn's life history would never be the same. The events following February 8, 1994, completely altered her perspective. She now referred to her existence as either BA and AA... Before Accident and After Accident.

Meanwhile, after Lynn was discharged and Janet continued to stop by the house on a daily basis, her training as an LPN kicked in. She wouldn't stay long but checked to see that home health nurses were present and caring for the patient. Basically, she wanted to see with her own two eyes that everything on the home front was up to her specifications. Janet was so involved with the task of orchestrating Lynn's recovery she forgot about her own maladies.

Days were followed by months. Summer vacation allowed Russ to be home with Lynn. Brooke began working as a clerk at Super One, a grocery store. She worked mostly evenings, and at that very grocery store, she met Matthew, who became her husband five summers later.

August arrived, and Lynn got back behind the wheel. For the first time since the accident, she drove the family car to her parents' house.

"Boy, it felt good to get in the car and not have to ask somebody to chauffeur me around town," Lynn told her mother.

Six months had passed. The family was settling back to a new normal when one night Russ woke up, gasped, and thought he was having a heart attack. Lynn called 911, and within minutes, several first responders arrived. Three of them were Lynn's cousins. They loaded Russ onto a stretcher and took his vitals while the girls looked on terror-stricken. Russ was rushed to the hospital where it was determined that he had a panic attack, not a heart attack.

Lynn's near death had taken its toll on her husband. Fortunately, Russ's anxiety was treatable, and the doctors outlined a plan for stress reduction with concentration on exercise and a healthier lifestyle.

One week later, Brooke left for her freshman year at the College of St. Benedict near St. Cloud. Robyn returned to her Snelling Avenue apartment and job as a retail store manager in Minneapolis, Russ began coaching football and two weeks later both he and Amy started another year back at Esko High School.

Therapy and doctor appointments consumed Lynn's life. In the fall of 1994, X-rays revealed that the right humerus was not fusing back together. Also, since the radial nerve had been severed near the fracture, the wrist hung limp and fingers were unable to grasp objects. Lynn needed yet another surgery.

Hand specialist, Dr. John Wood at the Mayo Clinic in Rochester, Minnesota, was enlisted to perform several procedures, while the patient was in the operating room. The humerus required new plating and bone grafting for the non-union and a tendon reconstruction was needed to hopefully correct radial nerve palsy.

A graft was harvested from the hip and the fractured humerus was secured for a second time with hardware. The radial nerve was reattached, but it was doubtful that the nerve would regenerate. That considered, three tendon transfers were performed to change flexors into extensors. A cumbersome cast with wires jutting out near the fingers gave Lynn the appearance of a freak robot. Yet, once the incisions healed and after many hours of occupational therapy and biofeedback, the procedures were deemed successful. Finally, Lynn was able to lift her wrist up and down and move her fingers. Unfortunately, numbness along the upper forearm never subsided. Yet on the plus side, the dominant right-handed woman regained the ability to write her name, a simple task once learned as a little girl with crooked bangs.

CHAPTER 43

It's A Wonderful Life

Seek first the kingdom of God and His righteousness,
and he will give you everything you need.
—Matthew 6:33 (NASB)

AMY LYNN HAD A HEAD full of dark shiny hair…a beautiful baby. Her parents wept at her birth, thanking God that she was healthy, no cleft palate from antiseizure medication or repercussions from Lynn's tubal ligation. The young mother worried about the prescription drugs she regularly took for petit mal epilepsy or how the anesthetic would affect the weeks-old fetus in her womb. She called on the Creator for help. God delivered. Amy Lynn was perfect, except for one thing: her duodenum was not fully developed. Needless to say, the little girl was a classic colic baby. Nothing relieved the tummy cramps that occurred just about every night from 7:00 p.m. until midnight.

Robyn and Brooke were able to sleep through the crying. Russ, on the other hand, was very stressed hearing the wailing baby. One evening, he ran out onto the backyard and began pulling blades of grass up by the roots. Uncle Howard from next door saw the frustrated dad.

"Hey, Russie boy, what the heck are you doing?" he hollered from between the boundary of evergreen trees.

Embarrassed, Russ fibbed, "Oh, I'm checking for creeping Charlie here in the backyard."

"Why don't you come over here and see if I have any?" Howie smiled to himself at his feeble invitation.

"Sure," Russ replied as he walked toward his neighbor's yard.

But instead of finding creeping Charlie in the neighbor's lawn, Russ placed his hands on a cold glass filled with Jack and Coke. "Ahhhh, thanks, Howie, you're a pretty good neighbor. When I need ya, you're always there for me."

Russ confessed how he felt just awful when Amy cried and cried.

The older man offered a tidbit of advice to the younger man.

"Soon it'll pass, and you'll forget all about it."

Six months later, baby Amy's tear-filled evenings ceased, and she became the delight of everyone.

The years rolled over one after another like the waters flowing under the Midway bridge…sometimes swiftly in a strong current after a flood, other times lazily pooling along the stagnant edges. As the children grew older, they became involved in girls' sports, including basketball, softball, volleyball, and cheerleading. Their father volunteered by coaching, while their mother actively fundraised.

When cousin Warren sold Lynn his baby grand piano, the three daughters took lessons for many years. Gymnastics and ballet added to the after-school activities. But when it was all said and done, dad's higher priority remained steadfast on their studies and academic achievement.

There was never a doubt the girls would pursue a post-secondary education. Russ referred to high school as "pretend" school. The girls understood continuing their education was mandatory. Although men's salaries were still higher than women's with similar job descriptions, the gender pay gap was narrowing. Still, in order to become employable in education, health care, or business, the Davidson girls needed college degrees. And that was that!

Lynn thought about returning to college but instead opened her own hair salon. During the summer of '79, Russ partitioned off a corner of the basement for the Snip and Clip Hair Boutique. Lynn ordered equipment, supplies, and flooring. Russ's grandpa John built a cabinet to house the shampoo bowl. For wall coverings, Ray furnished old barn board from a shed on a Meadowbrook field. A large mirror no longer needed by Aunt Bernice fit perfectly above the station. It was a family undertaking with many relatives helping to make the small business a reality. Once the shop was ready, newspaper advertisements announced the opening. Many clients followed Lynn from the Red Carpet in Cloquet to Esko.

Hours of operation were Wednesdays and Fridays from 9:00 a.m. to 5:00 p.m., Thursday from noon until 8:00 p.m. by appointment. During the school year, both Grandma Jackie and Grandma Millie babysat on alternate Fridays. Lynn made the decision to employ a nanny to come to the house and watch the girls on Wednesdays and Thursdays. A dear Christian woman Dorothy answered the call and was hired. The girls were showered with love and attention by Dorothy, who also baked cookies with the children and prepared meals for the family. Once summer vacation arrived, Russ assumed the babysitting role on days Lynn worked in the beauty shop.

The additional income from the Snip and Clip Hair Boutique helped the family budget remain solvent but also served as a positive outlet for Lynn. Making people look better made Lynn feel better. She learned to be a good listener and kept confidential information to herself. Throughout the twelve years of operation, the little basement salon became a place where clients became Lynn's friends.

Another outlet where friendships developed was through Community Bible Study. Lynn was active in CBS for twelve years serving as a core group leader for eight. Not affiliated with any church or denomination, each thirty-week course concentrated on home study questions, a core group discussion, lecture, and commentary. Unknowingly Jane, the director, played a valuable role as a mentor. Not only did Lynn study the scriptures, she also studied this lovely woman, who was godly, knowledgeable, and charming. Jane was yet another woman who had a lasting influence on Lynn.

CHAPTER 44

The Little Log House in the Woods

The quiet rhythmic monotone of a wall of logs fills one
with the rustic peace of a secluded nook in the woods.
—Gustav Stickley

IN THE AUTUMN OF 1977, Ray and Millie vacationed with friends, Clifford and Eilene. Their motorhome took them down to Missouri near the Ozark Mountains. The route twisted and turned through scenic byways promising breathtaking views. Along the way, Ray and Millie noticed magnificent log houses and smaller log cabins. The couple began talking about going home to Minnesota and building one. The two rationalized that they were nearing retirement and should downsize. Besides, they liked the novelty and look of old-fashioned logs.

Once in Esko, Ray and Millie studied various log house plans and decided on a complete kit that fit their specifications. The logs were harvested from Montana and trucked to the construction company located in Wisconsin. By spring the site was prepared and a cement slab was poured on the vacant lot where Mamie's trailer once sat.

Originally, Lynn appeared nostalgic and hated to see her parent's home sold to complete strangers. Much like Edwin A. Juntunen, Ray usually had a plan to help out his family. He asked daughter Janet if she wanted to buy the family home. Without reservation, she and

Dan agreed to Ray's plan, listed their house on Riverside Road, and sold it within a few weeks. They moved lock, stock, and barrel into the house where Janet had grown up playing "Queen for a Day" in the bathroom with her little sister. Now she was happily raising sons at that very same address.

Once his mind was made up, Ray was on a mission. Before long a quaint two-bedroom log cabin with a loft was erected under the guidance of brother-in-law Leo. Dan borrowed his company's crane and lifted the heavy center beam in place. From time to time friends and family stopped by; Uncle Hjalmer wasn't called upon to float the couple a loan, but still checked on the progress practically every day. Millie stained logs and woodwork. But this time around, she learned her lesson and she stayed off the steep roof while the house was shingled. Meanwhile, Lynn helped out as best she could by running errands or baking goodies for the crew.

When the log house was completed with new furnishings in place, Lynn's girls begged to play "Little House on the Prairie" over at Grandpa and Grandma's. They slept in the loft like the Ingall's sisters and played for hours in the back yard playhouse Grandpa Ray built for them. Millie planted a perennial flower garden, lilac bushes, two Honeycrisp apple trees, while Ray tilled the soil in preparation to grow potatoes, beans, and corn the following summer.

The dense log walls kept the house cool in the summer, while a Franklin wood stove warmed Ray and Millie during the winter. The laundry room on the main floor allowed the woman of the manor easy access for her Monday morning clothes washing ritual.

The couple lived for thirty years in the little log house nestled among the tall fir trees. But a dramatic shift occurred when early on a hot August morning, Millie discovered her husband unresponsive in their bed. The ambulance arrived to transport Ray to the hospital. But he died en route, less than a quarter of a mile from his birthplace, the same road where he and Grandpa Joseph lost control of the work horses and flew out of the wagon.

Raymond Donald was born in the farmhouse on the Juntunen Road and he died eighty-eight years later just down the road on the land he loved as much as his grandfather Joseph.

After her husband passed away it became apparent that Mildred couldn't live by herself in the log house. For six months her family cared for their mother, who was stricken with lewy body dementia. Then in January a fall and broken femur forced her to forever leave the log house. After being hospitalized for eight weeks of physical therapy, Millie transferred to Barnes Care, a newly built assisted/ memory care facility in Esko where she lived for eight years mostly in her own world. The anguish of watching "Wonder Woman" fade away left the family wondering "how long must Millie be here in body when she is absent in mind." Rarely did she recognize her children or grandchildren and her personality drastically changed. Lynn grieved the death of her mother long before she passed away. Yet, once in awhile for a fleeting moment, she'd come back to them like a fluttering butterfly landing on a flower. They wanted so desperately for the butterfly to stay. But without warning she would leave them with only a fond remembrance.

Mildred's son and daughters, along with countless family members and friends, visited Barnes Care never knowing what state her mind would be in. Yet, out of love and loyalty, they routinely stopped by for a few minutes and then left. They hoped their conversation might slow down the progression of the dreaded dementia. Then finally one January afternoon as the sun dipped into the western horizon, Millie closed her eyes. When she open them again, she saw the Lord face to face. Mother Fannie was smiling as father John placed a white peppermint candy into her hand and said, "Welcome home."

CHAPTER 45

The New Normal

If anyone is in Christ, he is a new creation;
the old has gone, the new has come!
—II Corinthians 5:17 (NIV)

BEFORE THE FOURTH-QUARTER SALES KICKED off, Avon regional manager Kathye phoned Lynn, inquiring about her progress and last appointment with the doctor. Once given the long-range diagnosis, Avon Corporation concurred that a replacement for the district manager position was necessary.

Although the determined woman had survived a horrendous car accident and was making great strides, Lynn could not return to the position she once held. The job description with long rigorous days traveling to Chicago and throughout northwest Wisconsin was too demanding and strenuous.

Lynn needed to explore other options and sought the advice of an attorney. There was no doubt she qualified for Avon's long-term disability plan and was granted Social Security Disability Income as well.

Yet at only forty-two years old, she needed to accept new limitations. This was not an easy transition. In her mind and heart, she believed she could do just about everything she had done prior to February 8, 1994. Unfortunately, her right leg and ankle hindered mobility. Orthopedic specialists offered a solution to fuse the ankle. Lynn refused sighting proof that she ambulated just fine, thank you. Pain became a constant reminder of the accident.

She was overly conscious of the large scars on her body as well as the fact that she walked with a wobbly gait. The right side was weakened. Stamina decreased and insomnia increased.

Lynn underwent counseling for post-traumatic stress. She suffered with extreme anxiety as a passenger in any vehicle. She preferred to be behind the wheel especially if snowflakes filled the air and accumulated.

Her friend "arthir" became a permanent resident in her body as arthritis found a home in joints. Exercising in a warm therapy pool helped keep muscles flexible and strong. Proper diet and adequate rest were new requirements to heal the body.

Recovery was slow and arduous. Yet Lynn tried to believe that her life still had purpose. There was a reason God spared her. As years followed, she was asked to tell her story and speak to various women's groups. The fact that she had been hit "head-on" by a woman named Grace was remarkable in itself. Instead, Lynn Rae was hit "head-on" by the grace of God, and for the time being, death had been averted—her life spared.

CHAPTER 46

Tell The Story

Let the redeemed of the Lord tell their story – those
he redeemed from the hand of the foe.
—Psalm 107:2 NIV

Oh give thanks to the Lord, call upon His name.
Make known His deeds among the peoples.
—I Chronicles 16:8 (NASB)

THE HIGH SCHOOL SWEETHEARTS, WHO wed so young, defied all odds. Their love and marriage stood the test of time while their daughters, no longer children, stood on their own. One by one, each of the girls graduated from college, becoming gainfully employed and off the Davidson payroll.

Sometimes, in the wee hours of the morn, when Lynn lay awake, she wondered what her life would've been like had not the fateful car accident occurred during the winter of '94. Russ, as well as their daughters, changed as a result, and so had she.

For starters, a deeper devotion bonded them to one another. "Family" had always been important because of the rich relationship fostered with grandparents, aunts, uncles, and cousins. Holidays centered around them. Had they taken those relationships for granted, assuming that they'd always be there?

Might Lynn's marriage been strained by the stress of working long hours, often out of town? Could her daughters have been sympathetic to those victimized by tragedy? Would Lynn have been able to relate to handicapped people? As providence would have it, those questions were no longer relevant.

Time marched on as did the family. In a span of five years all three daughters married wonderful men. Two were brothers Matthew and Peter, while Steve became the last guy to join the trio. Russ was elated to have "sons" to hang out with. In elegant style the couples made vows before God at the church with receptions for three-hundred guests at the Greysolon Ballroom in downtown Duluth. The evenings concluded with dancing and merriment. The father of the bride half-heartedly offered the option to bypass the traditional day with elopement and a check. All three told their dad, "No thanks!" a decision he expected. In the end, Russ shut his mouth and let the women orchestrate three separate wedding weekends: Brooke and Matt in '99, Amy and Peter in 2002, followed by Robyn and Steve in 2004. After the dust settled grandchildren began to enter the scene.

First to arrive was Jackson in 2003 on Minnesota Education Association (MEA), weekend in October. As an early Christmas gift, Maxwell entered the world in December of '05, followed by Samuel during a hot August day in '06. Then Nolan surprised everybody in '07 when he decided to suddenly meet his mother and dad in the bathroom at their home! After four grandsons, the Davidsons were blessed with a beautiful baby girl, Sophia Renee, who blew in with a snowstorm on the last month of 2007. Nathaniel Peter was born three months later.

Each child added a new dimension to the family with their unique personalities and special gifts. The creation of six grandbabies in four and a half years filled Grandma Lynn's heart with abounding joy that bubbled over like a babbling brook by the meadow.

The girl with the crooked bangs was no longer a child. She was a survivor, who inherited from her family strength and tenacity when faced with life's challenges. Their actions paved the way for Lynn and opened doors to new possibilities.

Being hit head-on by Grace Harris almost lead to an end, a sudden death for the middle aged woman. On the contrary, the accident opened the door to a more abundant, grace-filled life. She gleaned new insight into the goodness of humanity. No matter what negative messages the media relentlessly presented, after February 8, 1994, she and her family lived out a different more positive story. At times this was very difficult, because worry and fear bombarded their minds. But somehow, some way, the powerful Presence intercepted the negative self-talk. They attempted to be more aware of the moments and acknowledged a dependence on and strength through God.

There is power in the blood. Lynn's ancestors understood. The superstitious Sami relatives believed that reindeer blood sprinkled on a door warded off evil. The Bible taught her when Jewish men applied lamb's blood over the doorposts, the angel of death "passed over" their house, sparing the male children inside. Then, in the latter nineteenth century, a spiritual movement of Christianity, first revealed by the Finnish preacher, Levi Laestadian, taught Lynn's forefathers to believe that the blood of Jesus, covered the stain of sin, cleansing a heart from all unrighteousness.

Since then, God's amazing grace freed Lynn's family from strict rules and pagan ritual that stifled creativity and individual expression. The burden of measuring good works in order to compensate the bad never worked. How much was enough? Grace allowed them to be free to be exactly who God made them to be…the mission no longer impossible.

Lynn understood her mission evolved from the women who had come before her. Elsa Pykkonen braved the Atlantic Ocean in the squalor of a steamer. Although homesick for Finland, she knew she belonged in America.

Fannie Carlson Sunnarborg survived asphyxiation from a gas motored washing machine. She was discovered unconscious on the cement floor but revived to live until the age of eighty-eight. Mildred challenged herself in midlife by joining the Women's Movement and going back to school, discovering a new career. And even with a lifetime of illness and pain, Janet showed Lynn how to move beyond herself to comfort cancer victims at Hospice. Then there was mother-in-law Jackie, who courageously fought breast cancer and beat it.

These women left a giant footprint for Lynn to walk in. Even through the trials of daily life, they continued to raise the bar and offered their best to family, friends, and community.

A story lived within them. It was awaiting birth. But it involved struggle, pain, "*sisu.*" Then finally at the proper time, the story began to flow out from the little girl, *pikku tyttö*, who lived to tell it.

*****

Within four months, Lynn buried her ninety-seven-year-old mother and sister, Janet who lived until the age of seventy-two. These deaths left a gaping chasm in her life. Both had mothered Lynn, as she grew from the little girl with crooked bangs, to becoming a young mother with three daughters, to owning a small business, to competing in the marketplace as a district sales manager, to fighting for her life. They rejoiced in Lynn's success. They were her cheerleaders. They were always "there" for her.

No longer could she sit near them and share her story; therefore, it had to be written for her descendants.

She thought about Joseph and Elsa, Erick, and the Carlsons. She remembered the stories of their bravery. Lynn thought of the turbulent crossing, the seasickness, dysentery, and how many passengers on the ship never survived. Destiny led them across the Atlantic Ocean seeking freedom and a better way of life, not only for themselves but for their families and generations to follow.

She thought how they sacrificed and worked several jobs in order to save enough money to purchase land in America. Owning land signified prosperity, and Joseph instilled in his eldest son Andrew Edwin and grandson Raymontti this ideology.

In turn, the Maaranens (Carlsons) left the Sami tribe in northern Finland. Their nomadic culture was abandoned for planting in one place and establishing roots on American soil. Likewise, when Erick forced his son to either purchase the family farm or move, John and Fannie took the high road. The couple paid full price for the homestead, and figuratively speaking, fixed the bump in the road.

Shortly thereafter, the township identified the access into their property as the Sunnarborg Road

Lynn's forefathers and mothers not only dreamed of the day when they would finally achieve fulfillment, they took steps to reach that dream. They didn't fantasize about future happiness, while sands trickled away in an hourglass. They took action, one moment at a time. They experienced sorrow and tragedy, as well as joy and prosperity, yet never lost their focus, their purpose.

The little girl with the crooked bangs understood her rich heritage, because now she could look back upon her life. As a child, she walked upon the farmland and along the Midway River. She sat beneath the tall fir trees at the teepee and heard the whisper of God.

As a teen, she was carefree and at the same time careless. Yet, the girl, being chiseled by her Creator, as well as, her own decision-making, discovered young love to last a lifetime.

As mother, she accepted the role well aware of the fact that she could not raise children on her own power. And even with a husband's support, Lynn understood her limitations. She needed a Helper to direct her steps while nurturing three daughters. In addition, her mother, mother-in-law, sister, aunts, grandmothers, along with women employers and friends notably influenced her.

In midlife, she stepped out of her comfort zone and bravely faced a new career. Avon's divisional manager Kathye challenged Lynn to meet and exceed goals. She thrived in the business world and looked forward to a promising future with the company, only to have those aspirations crash.

On February 8, 1994, death attempted to destroy her dreams. A woman named Grace could have robbed Lynn of fulfilling her destiny. For that brief moment, she believed that she was dying…her life ending, her husband a widower, her children without a mother, her last wishes expressing love for them.

However, God's amazing Grace pulled the woman out from the wreckage, pulled her through countless surgeries and unrelenting pain, and pulled her back to discovering her heritage.

For in the little township near the head of Lake Superior, the place where Finnish ancestors settled, a bond held fast. The bond would never be broken, because it was cemented in love and loyalty to family, friends, and community. There was no exclusivity or partiality that determined who benefited. When trouble came knocking or hardship crumbled a life, the residents came to each other's rescue. They raised a new barn, when one burnt and solicited funds for the cancer victim. They sympathized with the family whose child drowned. They supported school activities and celebrated victories. Brother helping brother. Sister helping sister.

That was the modus operandi, M.O. of the people in the small community. That was the heritage the woman wanted her children to understand and hoped that heritage would live on and on and on.

EPILOGUE

THE WOMAN, NEARLY EIGHTY YEARS old, shuffled along the wooden sidewalk near the Aerial Lift Bridge at the Port of Duluth-Superior. Screeching gulls floated through the air, waiting patiently for a food scrap to fall from a tourist's hand.

Down by the harbor a gentle breeze lightly kissed the wrinkled cheek…reminiscent of her husband's soft caress. Waves washed over the rocky shoreline, ebbing and flowing to the beat of her heart. Lynn paused for a moment remembering…

"Oh, how she had loved the man and that love grew deeper and wider than the roots of the oak tree in their front yard. She'd known at sixteen that he was "the one."

As a child, God whispered to her while she sat at the teepee fort in the meadow and brook. But the days of romping through the woods were gone.

Instead, she walked along with a cane clutched in hand. She needed it most days to steady herself. The leg that sustained so many fractures forty years ago was weak and arthritic. But the woman was determined as always. She laughed out loud remembering how she had insisted on walking for Brooke's graduation…one step at a time.

That was exactly how Joseph and Elsa, Erick, and the Carlsons walked onto the shores of Lake Superior, taking one step at a time. Their life steps changed their destiny for a new freedom with greater possibilities. The woman pondered what might have happened if her great-grandparents had remained in Finland. But they hadn't. Destiny and God led them across the ocean, to New York harbor to Michigan, and finally to the shores of Gitchi Gumi.

They dared to alter their course, to risk making mistakes, yet learn from them. They were pilgrims in progress, who undeniably changed the direction of their lives and in turn, the fate of their heirs.

Over the woman's lifetime, countless changes occurred in Esko's landscape. No longer a farming community, plots of land were developed for housing making it a very desirable bedroom community. With the completion of Interstate 35, traffic was diverted away from Esko's Corner.

The Co-op store was now a pizza parlor. Juntti's Fairway Food Store changed ownership three times. Eventually the building was demolished and replaced with a dental office. The Dairy Delight became an accounting office and Rog's Galley drive-in was converted into an insurance office. RAM Insurance emerged as the major employer in the township, other than Independent School District #99. The school remained the centerpiece at Esko's Corner with enrollment soaring because of its academic excellence.

The woman sighed deeply as she thought about the past. Memory loss was frightening, and it was slowly happening to her. Yet, she didn't want to live in the past, nor fear the future. She wanted to wrap her arms around the present and embrace it with a bear hug.

Her eyes squinted from the bright reflection the sun cast over the deep water. She stood for several minutes gazing at the beauty of the clear, blue-gray waves before her legs begged to rest. A nearby bench was the perfect place to be still. And there she sat quietly with her thoughts. They were interrupted by grandson Nate, who just finished jogging along the boardwalk.

He had a couple days off and had driven up from the Twin Cities. Grandma Lynn asked him to take her to Duluth and to the harbor. Since they both loved the lakeshore, she deemed it unlikely he'd say "No." Besides, Nate could never refuse her requests.

As he joined her on the bench, he looked down and noticed shiny glass.

"Hey Gramma, look what's under the bench?

A quart Mason jar held an elongated chrysalis attached to a small branch. Someone had placed it in a jar for safe keeping, but then forgot it.

"Look, Gramma, it's moving."

"Don't touch it, Nate. We don't want to interfere with its meta-morphosis. Keep it in the jar and we'll take it home."

The woman believed that butterflies represented new life and resurrection and that a visit by one could be a sign from a guardian angel.

Once they got back to the house in Esko, the woman left the jar on the kitchen counter and soon forgot about it. She fed her grandson a light supper and he decided to drive back home. His daughter would still be awake. Nate could end the day by reading her a bedtime story.

The old woman was tired from the outing and all the fresh air. Once Nate left, she began her nightly ritual. After changing into a pink flannel nightgown, she washed her face, wishing the wrinkles would slide off into the sink. Then she realistically patted on Olay age-defying cream, and brushed her pearly whites. She filled a water glass, then swallowed in one gulp her nightly meds. Lynn crawled into bed and shut off the bedside lamp. Before the frogs started croaking a nightly serenade in the pond, sleep came softly.

While Lynn slept the monarch butterfly fluttered in the dark place in its comfort and safety. She resisted God's natural force to push herself out from within the cocoon. She did not understand that, with each movement, she was freeing herself—until, suddenly, the outer shell broke from the top, and slowly she emerged to begin a new life. She hung upside down on the branch drying the orange, and black wings, as blood flowed through them, making them strong enough to fly south to Mexico next winter.

This butterfly was one of the fortunate. The species was threat-ened since natural habitat of milkweed, the host plant, as well as, nectar plants for nourishing the adults were diminishing. Her life was spared and the monarch had a destiny.

*****

In the morning, the woman woke up feeling refreshed. She got out of bed, stretched both arms and legs, then slowly made her way

241

to the kitchen. After filling the carafe with water, she reached for the coffee grounds in the cabinet above the counter. Then she gasped.

An exquisite monarch butterfly rested on the branch inside the Mason jar. Quickly she phoned Nate before he left for work.

"Hi Gramma, is anything wrong?" Usually she didn't call him this early.

"No, Nate. Guess what I discovered on the counter this morning? The caterpillar's shell cracked and is empty and the loveliest monarch butterfly quietly rests in the jar. I'll take a picture and send it to you."

"Ahh Gram, that's great. I'll look for the text and picture. Thanks for calling. I had fun at Canal Park yesterday."

"Me, too, Nate! You and your family are welcome here anytime. Bye!"

A week later Gramma Lynn invited all six grandchildren to come for dinner at her house in Esko. Two lived nearby, while the other four carpooled from the Twin Cities. The matriarch was thankful that the grandchildren shared many fond memories of being together. The bond of blood flowed through the six cousins in a circle that remained unbroken. Even with extremely busy schedules, they knew attendance was compulsory. Gramma didn't convene a meeting unless it was very important.

By four o'clock everyone had arrived and was starving. Despite the fact they were all in their thirties, remembrances of Gramma's home cooking made their mouth's water. She promised not to disappoint. First, her guests munched on crunchy taco cups topped with sour cream and cilantro. Homemade corn salsa and chips were served with a pitcher of margaritas. For the entrée, the elderly woman prepared chicken enchiladas with a generous dollop of sour cream and guacamole. They groaned with delight when tequila cheesecake bars and freshly ground cinnamon coffee topped off the meal.

Everyone helped by clearing the table and loading the dishwasher, while Gramma watched in admiration. After the kitchen was spotless, the old woman summoned the grandchildren to be seated in the living room, and once there began her spiel.

"You know how much our little town has meant to Papa and me. Not only were we raised here, your 3rd great grandparents settled in Thomson Township as early as 1885. The stories of your heritage must live on. The only way that will happen is if you continue to pass down our legacy. Now today the baton is in your hand. It's up to you. Don't let me down.

I have had a wonderful life. Forty years ago when I was in a car accident, I thought I was dying. Do you know what was my last request? Love...tell my girls that I love them. That is what I ask of you. Over and over again, tell your children that you love them.

Throughout my eighty-plus years, I've made mistakes along the way...said things I've regretted. I've had to ask God and others to forgive me. I hope you are never too proud to admit when you're wrong. Even if you're not sure, be like Raymond and say, "Maybe it was part my fault, I'm sorry." Your lives will enjoy more peace and less controversy.

Benjamin Franklin first said, "Honesty is the best policy." That is still true today. Don't think you can cheat others and not be found out. You reap what you sow, and God will know.

Debt is one of the most dangerous four-letter words. Don't believe the lie that promises fulfillment with possessions. You will only want more and greed may grip your heart.

Work hard and you will be rewarded. Setting goals and achieving them will give you immense satisfaction. However, don't make the mistake of placing the demands of your career before the needs of your family.

Preserve the family unit. Even though you have great friends, remember "from whence you came." Your family will love you unconditionally and forgive you. Blood is a powerful bond to loyalty.

Like in the game of Monopoly, you can use the Free Pass – Go Home. Some day we all will come face to face with the Creator and we will have to give an account of our lives. Like me, you will have fallen short, because we aren't perfect. The only one who was perfect was Jesus and he made the final sacrifice of blood. And that blood is our pass to heaven.

Believe John 3:16 (NASB). It is the foundation of Christianity. "For God so loved the world (me) that he gave his only son (Jesus) that whoever believes in him, will not perish, but have everlasting life."

Now follow me out onto the deck. We're ending this party with a new release."

The entourage of six followed their grandmother outside. In her hand was the Mason jar and in the jar was the monarch butterfly. They encircled the old woman and watched closely as she unscrewed the lid. With gnarled fingers she tapped the clear bottom and waited.

"Come on now, lovely monarch, you're free!"

As if the butterfly heard the prompt, her vibrant wings delicately fluttered and lifted her out from the jar. Up, up, up, she climbed into the eastern sky, then glided down to rest on the petals of a black-eyed Susan. The butterfly blended with the hue of the flower until its wings ever so slightly flitted up and down.

"Now every time you see a butterfly, it will be a reminder that a guardian angel is watching over you, my dear and precious grandchildren."

The moment was interrupted when the phone rang. It was for Sophia. Her mother wanted to know if she was spending the night. No, but thanks. She was carpooling back to Minneapolis with her three cousins.

A farewell of hugs and kisses bid them adieu with a final "I love you" for good measure.

The house resumed a quietness Lynn was now accustomed to. She thought about the meeting and was thankful it had gone so well. How imperative to the old woman that this session occurred. Finally the nightly ritual concluded with prayers asking God to watch over her family. Now she could rest in peace.

Yet, sleep evaded her that night, perhaps caused from all the extra excitement of the day.

Oh well, she thought, I can nap tomorrow.

Lynn tossed and turned in the fluffy comforter for another hour, punched twice her down pillow, then finally faded off to sweet dreams.

The next morning the phone rang and rang at the house on Memorial Drive. No one answered.

The woman was discovered lying peacefully in the queen bed, that once upon a time she shared with her king. During the early morning, her heart had stopped. It had pumped flawlessly for over eighty years. Now its work was done.

True to form, she left final instructions for her family. Even after death, she still was telling them what to do! Lynn Rae's body was cremated, and a memorial service was held on a balmy August day. A turkey dinner with all the trimmings was served to everyone in attendance.

Half of the ashes were buried in the family cemetery plot next to her husband's. Calla lilies, hydrangeas, and white roses were laid beside the broken earth. They were reminiscent of the flowers each daughter carried on their wedding day.

The other half of the matriarch's ashes was tossed over the Meadowbrook swimming hole near the place where the wooden bridge once crossed over the pasture. As a child she walked the land where Joseph and Elsa first settled, singing the song from the movie, "The Exodus."

"This land is mine, God gave this land to me." The spirited girl's spirit was now in the Promised Land.

A strong current swirled the remaining ashes into the river water, circling round and round until suddenly they were no more.

The little girl with crooked bangs had come full circle.

About the Author

LYNN RAE DAVIDSON TELLS THE story of a rich heritage and survival from a head-on car accident. As the daughter of a dairy farmer, teacher's wife, and mother of three girls, she weaves the story of life along with lessons of love, rejection, resilience, and acceptance.

Her career as a businesswoman included owning a full-service hair salon, being employed as a marketing executive for an advertising agency and managing a district of 325 representatives for Avon Corporation. Her entrepreneurial and leadership skills were honed as Lynn volunteered with nationally acclaimed Community Bible Study as a core group leader and initiated and chaired the school district's first All-Night Graduation Party. She was active on her church board, VBS, and choir. This is her first book inspired by real-life events.

CPSIA information can be obtained
at www.ICGtesting.com
Printed in the USA
LVHW112246010519
616347LV00001B/144/P